'*Get Productive!* by Magdalena Bak-~~~~~~ment' book. Instead, the book focus~~~~and enjoy the results you really care ~~~~insightful examples and provocative ideas, this book will help you achieve the balance and results you want.'

Steven D'Souza, Executive Fellow, IE Business School, Author of Brilliant Networking, *www.brilliantnetworking.net*

'This is the most practical book on productivity I have ever read. The thing I love most about it is the fact you don't have to read it from the first until the last page to get the help you need. This book has a perfect set of exercises you can take at any point in your life to get organized, be more productive and generally get more out of your life. As a leader of a global organization, I wish I'd been able to read this book at the start of my term and run those exercises with my team to get the most out of each individual. No matter what you do, where you work or how old you are, I recommend this book for reading and exercising your productivity.'

Tetiana Mykhailiuk, President of AIESEC International, www.aiesec.org

'A brilliantly practical step-by-step handbook for ultimate productivity. This book will boost your energy and time a hundred fold. A must-read for all those who want to live and work smarter, not harder.'

Suzy Greaves, author of Making The Big Leap *and named as a 'top ten guru to change your life around' by* The Daily Mail

'*Get Productive!* is an excellent practical book that lives up to its stated objectives, namely how to become more productive within a holistic framework. By considering productivity in its many forms, the reader is given relevant exercises and understanding to develop the skills required to lead a more fulfilling and productive life whether personal or professional.'

Gladeana McMahon, FAC, FBCAP, FISMA, FRSA – UK Chair Association for Coaching

'In her book, *Get Productive!*, Magdalena Bak-Maier has assembled over 30 techniques for improving an individual's effectiveness that really work! She has used her background in neuroscience combined with her career experience as a consultant and coach to significant effect and will help readers gain valuable productivity insights. The producer and eggs; diamonds, gold and lead; goal clarifying;

assumptions in conversations; the action funnel; bursts and lags are some of my favourite. I wholeheartedly recommend this book.'

Peter Childs, FRSA, FIMechE, FASME, PhD, BSc, CEng – Professorial Lead in Engineering Design and Innovation Design Engineering Joint Course Director – Imperial College London, Royal College of Art

'Packed with simple, effective and easy to use tips, this is a book with the power to change the bad habits of a lifetime! So much more than good time management, *Get Productive!* will create powerful awareness through easy exercises and coach you to uncover your blocks. A small investment in time will see you acting immediately towards positive changes. The tips and tools can be easily transferred to support team performance, ensuring they focus on value-adding activities and maximise their impact on internal and external stakeholders.

There are lessons for life as well as work; encouraging and empowering us to focus on our WANTs over the MUSTs and effectively matching tasks to energy levels. We all have energy drainers in our lives, now we can identify and reduce them to increase performance, productivity and positivity!'

Karen Dempsey, Head of HR UK & Ireland for Air France KLM

'*Get Productive!* is a powerful, practical toolkit for a complex, fast changing world. It coaches in a holistic and integrated way, seeking balance in everything that matters. Written by a master practitioner and based on proven experience in real businesses, I am using techniques from *Get Productive!* both personally and with my team to deliver results.'

Jon Tucker, Operating Officer, Imperial College Business School

'Whatever you strive for in life, you are far more likely to achieve if you can use your time, your skills and your energy more effectively. Magdalena is a master at focusing ambitions, refining aspirations and making each re-energised step feel both possible and thrilling. *Get Productive!* distils her considerable insights and expertise in an easy-to-use format which will be a huge help in whatever you aspire to do. What shines through the book is that many of the obstacles that lie in our path are of our own imagining, and with this book in our hand, that need no longer be the case.'

Rob Hopkins, Transition Network and Author of The Transition Companion

'Packed full of practical, insightful exercises, supercharging your energy to power through any productivity roadblocks.'

Guy Browning, The Guardian

GET PRODUCTIVE!

Boosting Your Productivity and Getting Things Done

Magdalena Bak-Maier

CAPSTONE

This edition first published 2012
© 2012 Magdalena Bak-Maier
Author photo: © Phine Ka Photography

Registered office
Capstone Publishing Ltd. (A Wiley Company), John Wiley and Sons Ltd, The Atrium, Southern Gate, Chichester, West Sussex, PO19 8SQ, United Kingdom

For details of our global editorial offices, for customer services and for information about how to apply for permission to reuse the copyright material in this book please see our website at www.wiley.com.

Library of Congress Cataloging-in-Publication Data
Bak-Maier, Magdalena, 1977–
   Get productive! : boosting your productivity and getting things done / Magdalena Bak-Maier.
      p.   cm.
   Includes index.
   ISBN 978-0-85708-346-3 (pbk.)
   1. Labor productivity.   2. Performance.   3. Time management.
4. Organizational effectiveness.   I. Title.
   HD57.B28   2012
   650.1'1–dc23
                                            2012022699
A catalogue record for this book is available from the British Library.

ISBN 978-0-857-08346-3 (pbk)   ISBN 978-0-857-08343-2 (ebk)
ISBN 978-0-857-08344-9 (ebk)   ISBN 978-0-857-08345-6 (ebk)

Set in 10/13.5 pt ACaslonPro-Regular by Toppan Best-set Premedia Limited
Printed in Great Britain by TJ International Ltd, Padstow, Cornwall, UK

This book is dedicated to those who value and commit to showing up in life with authenticity, courage and passion, those who want to share their skills/gifts with the world and to my parents.

CONTENTS

Contents

THE PERFECT STARTING POINT (IF YOU DON'T KNOW WHERE TO START)

TRUE PRODUCTIVITY

Imagine living your life's purpose and experiencing results beyond anything you dare to envisage; a way of being in the world that allows you to create what you want and inspire others to do the same. It is possible to be very efficient and yet still not be very productive. You might have great ideas and plans but never get around to implementing them. You might appear to be an accomplished, successful person but still question your own purpose or cry on the inside.

Many people tend to think that poor time management is the 'main' reason why they are unproductive. However, good time management doesn't always necessarily mean effective productivity – it's not just about trying to get things done in less time. Personal productivity is a holistic concept that is far broader than time management. True productivity is about being effective across many spectra: personal organization, effective thinking and decision making, the ability to be creative, flexible and resilient, good time management, the ability to communicate and get things done, a high degree of self-awareness and the ability to learn.

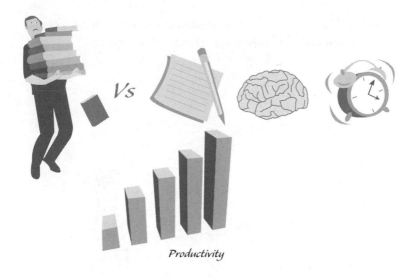

Productivity

Get Productive! is designed to help you develop your productivity in a holistic sense but without you having to read it from cover to cover. This book works by developing your skills of awareness, thinking and action to create better results in less time across all areas. It does not aim to give you answers. Instead, it provides you with exercises and methods to get you to work right away with your own material, challenges and context irrespective of your position, role or life circumstances.

A NEW APPROACH TO PRODUCTIVITY

In today's busy world, we all suffer from lack of time to step back and think. Our professional and personal lives are full of potential pressure cookers and awkward situations that require us to be productive quickly. In fact, as information grows at an unprecedented rate, we think less and less while the world around us becomes increasingly complex. The pace of technological advances and scientific discoveries outstrips our ability to cope unless we are subject experts.

Time-focused
productivity

Get productive!
Brain-focused
productivity!

We live in an exciting world but are starved of conventional wisdom. Our ability to learn, adopt and integrate our learning is compromised by the time-short and quick-results-demanding world. If we continue as we are, we risk burning out or playing constant catch up. This is not a desirable or productive way of being.

WHAT'S DIFFERENT ABOUT THIS BOOK?

Over the last two decades many business books and self-help guides have taken an approach that is based on telling you what to do. It makes sense. They give you tips and proven methods to help you address specific problems such as how to manage people, how to save time, how to communicate, negotiate or network. These days, when you have a problem there's a book out there to help address it. It's literally one Amazon click away, but the main challenge is finding time to read the wisdom contained within it. Few books, however, guide you in finding your own answers effectively. Learning only really works when you can put what you've read straight into practice to create new, effective habits.

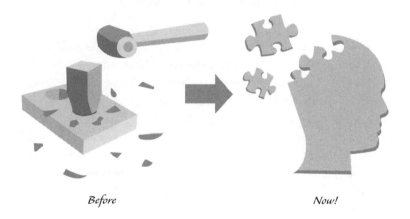

Before   *Now!*

Get Productive!, then, is about making time count: a personal philosophy that has emerged in my work developing others as well as in developing myself. It is about using common sense and proven techniques in combination with your best thinking to create practical solutions from the information you gain and facts you analyze. *Get Productive!* is grounded in practical ways of being and achieving results in a state of ease and play. Action is guided by effective reflection, integrative systems thinking and pure pragmatism married with honesty to work with what is *true* for you. No pretending. No trying to look good. Instead, you are at your best because you're working with your very best. When you own what you do one hundred percent, you do your best and in the process will achieve outstanding results in all areas of your life.

> *Your success =*
> *Top results on healthy terms*
> *based on learning,*
> *active thinking and action!*

The approach in this book involves learning about yourself, developing clarity about what you're passionate about, good at and what you want to create and then doing it right away. You can't contemplate being an effective and credible leader in today's world without modelling productivity yourself. And if you're running an organization or working in a team, your combined productivity is key to your overall performance. This means that in addition to being productive yourself, your job is to help create conditions where others can be productive too. Working with this book will help you do that. Countless managers, leaders, entrepreneurs and other professionals as well as fellow coaches and coaching clients have tried these approaches with me and found them useful.

Time has become one of the most precious commodities you have to sell, give and share. Yet because it is less tangible than other products, we often forget its true value. Hence, being productive is a key priority for individuals and organizations. Knowing how to make time count is a mindset shift and a fundamental skill that will help you create impact, make the most of your life and help you find satisfaction and success. It is good leadership modelled by example. *Yours.*

We live in very exciting times. Our lives have immense potential to be thrilling and rewarding. Your life and actions do matter! Think about famous leaders and change makers. They are not different from you and me. There is a lot to be done and a lot of things to be achieved. There is no better time than now to make a difference.

HOW TO USE THIS BOOK

This book takes a practical approach that reflects the way I like to work and how I have been able to work effectively with others over the last few years.

The book is divided into five sections, each containing a series of short, specific exercises. These exercises can be done in any order, as and when you need to. A short introduction to each exercise will provide you with a broad context for best application. Since you will be using your own material, what you will learn will help you to improve your productivity right away. Each exercise contains Reflective Questions that aim to develop your thinking skills and help ensure that you are considering your actions in sufficient context.

All the exercises use helpful visual tools, memorable frameworks and questions to guide you in developing answers for yourself, because you are the best judge of what will and won't work for you. The short chunks of time you invest in each exercise you choose to do will help you to identify practical solutions and implement specific improvements straight away in your work and life. This means you will save valuable time and get things done faster and better.

I would also suggest that you take notes in a way that suits your style and preference. Use a format that works effectively for you, whether that means a notepad and pen, an iPad, a phone, a nifty program or online tool. There is real mileage and magic in capturing your ideas in some form that allows you to take a step back and look at it in full. Seeing things in front of you helps you develop your thinking and will ensure that your actions are well considered and incorporate all the relevant information. You will also have an immediate and useful way to review and track your progress. At the end of each exercise you will find a set of broad Takeaway Lessons to encourage you to extract a certain level of information from each activity.

The various sections and exercises benefit from being revisited at different times. Therefore, there is no right or wrong way of interacting with this book. I would not advise you to work through the book from cover to cover in one sitting; instead, I invite you to be guided by your immediate needs. The insights generated in these activities are current and practical. With a certain incubation period and further reflection and integration, your thinking and approach to productivity will strengthen more and more.

Start with a section that's relevant for you. Be open-minded and trust yourself that whatever you do, the benefits of your actions will produce great results across your life and increase your happiness. Be bold and courageous. Work at your own speed. Be patient with yourself. The time you invest in this book will serve you well. Own the book and own the process.

I wish you lots of fun, happiness and wonderful results!

Magdalena Bak-Maier

1

FIND YOUR OWN PRODUCTIVITY BALANCE

What came first the egg or the chicken? Who cares! Both are key and interdependent. We can't have eggs without a chicken and chickens come from incubated eggs. If you think about the chicken as the producer of goods and the eggs as results, good eggs are made by healthy chickens. What is vital and yet often overlooked is the balance between the producer (you) and the product egg (the results you produce). A balance that *you* proactively manage rather than one that comes out of what's happening *to you*.

A vital part of success and productivity is taking care of the producer – you. When your needs are met, you'll be in a good place to perform at your best. If you feel safe and appreciated in the workplace, you're more likely to risk asking difficult but critical questions and are also likely to engage more. If you feel acknowledged and loved for who you are by your friends and family, you're more likely to be honest with them and you'll often go to great lengths to help. When you are truly productive, then, you can deliver results without wearing yourself down. In fact, delivering results will re-energize and sustain you.

Most people experience crunch times. Some people work through one crunch time after another until they literally burn out. The danger with spending all or most of your energy on egg production is that, at some point, you – the hen – will get tired, your wellbeing and satisfaction will suffer and you will become at risk of getting stressed out. You end up missing out on life's greatest pleasure – the joy of balance.

The following Product–Producer Balancer exercise is a quick, simple, practical and useful way to take stock of what needs your attention in the short, mid and longer term for maximal productivity that is truly sustainable. If you only focus on cranking out 'results', you put yourself at risk of burning out at some stage. On the other hand, if you focus solely on taking care of the producer, you might find that you're not pleased with your results, especially if you enjoy success and achieving.

Think of your overall productivity as the sum of two numbers – producer and product. If the producer is tired or weak, it is difficult if not impossible to create a great product. Equally, if what you make is not well thought out and the producer is capable of more, your overall result will be poorer than what you're capable of. Therefore, this exercise should help you to develop explicit awareness of how things are, pinpoint areas that may require minor or major tweaks and help you to acknowledge and celebrate your ability to keep a good balance. The exercise applies equally well in all contexts: job, career, life, relationship, role, project and so on.

PRODUCT–PRODUCER BALANCER EXERCISE

1. Imagine yourself as a healthy chicken that sits on a nest of wonderful, healthy eggs or a single healthy egg. The egg might be your fantastic job, healthy family, a well-conceived and executed project or an amazing partner. The healthy chicken is you in top mental, emotional, physical and spiritual form: you at your very best.

2. Use the following scale to rank the current health state of you – the chicken – and of each of your key eggs:
   Top health – excellent condition
   OK – could be improved
   Sickly – you know what's wrong and you know how to fix it
   Critical – needs attention right now or serious loss risk
   Dead – completely exhausted or lost

Dead   Critical   Sickly   OK   Top health

3. Assess where you – the chicken – fall along the scale, as well as each of your eggs. Do many fall towards the healthy end, or more towards the critical end?

   Notes:

4. Note where the focus is right now – is it on the product or the producer?

Notes:

 Reflective Questions

- What would top health/excellent condition look like for you? How would you feel? What could you achieve?
- If you look back in time, what does the product–producer balance look like for you? Is the balance appropriate or does the producer or product suffer? What most contributes to this situation? How can you ensure this does not repeat itself?
- What is the general trend? Are you getting better, staying the same or getting worse in maintaining a healthy balance?
- Looking forward, what would you like the balance to look like? What indicators/measures of success can you establish to help you keep track?

 FIND YOUR OWN PRODUCTIVITY BALANCE: TAKEAWAY LESSONS

Completing this exercise should help you assess your overall productivity at the moment in a way that pays attention to your wellbeing and balance. Having worked with many achievers and people with exceptional drive, I know from experience that being able to control and maintain good balance as producers is not easy. It is, however, possible. By examining what you pay more attention to, you can begin to create explicit awareness of effective habits and those that cause you to suffer and undermine your overall performance. A regular quick review of this exercise will certainly help you to see how you're doing. It's like a temperature gauge that lets you know if you're OK quickly.

If you find yourself lacking in good balance, you may wish to consider specific actions you could take to introduce better balance. If you find that your producer is suffering, for example, this often means paying more attention to your body, nutrition and creating rest time. Creating new habits may initially feel like you are doing more activities, but once introduced into your daily routine, these little 'producer maintainers', such as regular exercise, a short time out over a good cup of coffee or a phone call to someone you care about, can do wonders for your overall productivity. Many exercises in this book will explicitly help you identify ideas for taking care of the producer. Alternatively, you may wish to work with a qualified professional. If your producer is compromised, I do urge you to take action promptly, as a healthy producer is fundamental to your overall productivity.

If, however, you find that you are less than totally satisfied with the quality of your products (eggs), I would suggest a time-friendly review of your activities with specific exercises in this book such as the Diamond, Gold and Lead Exercise (Chapter 6) or the Goal Highlighter (Chapter 13) as a good starting point. Often what's needed is a slight refocus or minor shift that becomes obvious when you take the time to look at what is actually going on. You may also wish to work with someone else (a coach, mentor, therapist, colleague or friend) to help you think through what you hope to create. Whatever you decide, do not wait. Addressing your imbalance with action will automatically move you forward by creating a change.

Using your mind to observe, learn and ask questions as we do in this book will help you to find your own solutions for optimal productivity.

If you find yourself having perfect balance a lot, really take the time to celebrate! This is an important skill that will help ensure you remain grounded, successful and enjoy what you're doing. People who exhibit good balance help others do the same through example. Often they have specific benchmarks or references that help them know what good balance looks like from daily journals, mindful practices to tune in and self-check, regular reviews and fitness checks to name but a few. I remember a manager I once worked with who advocated good work–life balance and always left the office at 4:30 to pick up his children from school. His staff knew he believed and practised what he preached. He was also hugely successful. His behaviour demonstrated to others that success in terms of overall productivity meant good balance and he was at its centre.

Examining your overall balance sets you up for effective working and high-level personal productivity. If you work in a team or lead a team, you may wish to complete this exercise with others.

SECTION ONE
HELP! I'M JUST NOT GETTING ANYWHERE

Yep, this was me one day. I love journals and I'm never more than a metre away from one. They collect my thoughts, ideas, reflections and internal snippets of dialogue like this one: There are times when dark clouds of doubt show up over the horizon and I ask myself, 'Where is all my effort going?' and 'Am I really being productive?' Working with others, I quickly realized that I'm not alone. Whether you're running your own business, working for someone else, leading a team or out of work, there are distinct moments when it can feel like you expend loads and loads of energy, there's a long list of things to do staring at you and yet there are few tangible results to show for all your hard work. This is a critical time where productive people pause to notice, review and adjust while others lose motivation, continue to expend masses of energy without clear purpose or give up.

The exercises in this section will help you assess your energy, see how it is used at the moment and what might be blocking your overall productivity. You will develop your conscious awareness of how you spend time now and identify quick improvements you can implement straight away for quick bottom-line results. Make them part of your practice.

2

ASSESS YOUR ENERGY LEVELS

To be operating at your best and make good decisions, you need to have an appropriate level of energy. Imagine trying to run a race with blisters on your feet or performing at your best in a job interview when you have just received some bad news. To give and do your best, you have to be and feel at your best. Energy is fuel. Think of a time when you were totally excited, one hundred percent present, your mind was clear and ready and your heart open for whatever might come. You were in the zone.

Our energy can be divided into four types:

1. Physical – can I run another mile?
2. Mental – is my brain in the best state to think about this?
3. Spiritual – am I in alignment with my values and what's important to me?
4. Emotional – am I experiencing emotions that are draining my overall state or nurturing it?

I call these energy types the Four Cylinders. Each cylinder is connected with activities that help keep the energy at high levels. These can include things like nutrition, exercise, rest, learning, certain people, relationships, specific activities, interests and other wellbeing practices. It is worth thinking about specific behaviours and activities you can undertake to replenish energy for best performance. Depletion in any of the four cylinders will affect your overall wellbeing, how productive you can be, the results you deliver and how long you can sustain your performance at a consistently high level. When the energy levels get very low, you risk burn out.

Each task requires a certain combination of type and levels of energy. Knowledge about what you are like when you are full of energy, combined with awareness about the state of these energies at any given moment, is an important part of a strategy for being at your most productive. It allows you to match the energy you have with a given task. When you know your top priorities or goals, you can quickly assess whether you have the right levels of energy to tackle them with success, whether the goal needs to be broken down or your energy level raised.

Your mind routinely scans your energy levels anyway, although it probably happens without your conscious awareness. The brain sends various signals letting you know what it needs to help you perform at your best. It may tell you to rest, to get fresh air or to seek counsel. Most people, however, do not pay enough attention to their body, until the signal is difficult or impossible to ignore. Even when you find yourself working outside your comfort zone (i.e. things become uncomfortable or highly stressful), you will rarely think about your energy being depleted. Instead you are likely to take some action that will most quickly restore you to a higher level of energy: drinking more coffee, eating sugary foods or getting angry. Often in crutch situations these seemingly energy-restoring activities are, in fact, robbing you of top-level performance. Being effective means you take charge and responsibility for working at your true best and have healthy and effective strategies to keep yourself there at all times.

The Four Cylinders exercise is a quick and powerful method for developing awareness about energy so that you can channel it effectively for high productivity. It is based on a simple rating scale technique to help you understand your energy states.

When you are clear about your energy levels and the action you want to take, you can match tasks with energy levels or work to adjust your energy for a given task in a conscious way. Make the Four Cylinders part of your daily practice, especially when you have to undertake a demanding task but also when you simply want to check your own wellbeing and/or restore it.

FOUR CYLINDERS EXERCISE

1. Learning about your energy states

Think about something specific you achieved where you thought you worked at your best. It could be a presentation you gave, a course you mastered or a successful negotiation you pulled off. Given the four types of energy – physical, mental, emotional and spiritual – what level of energy in percentage terms did you have when you were at your best?

Notes:

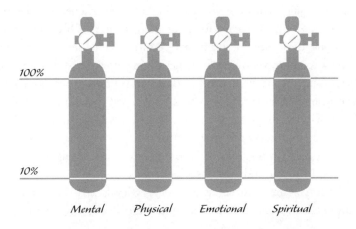

Mental   Physical   Emotional   Spiritual

2. **Present moment energy awareness**
   Now, tune into the present moment and give yourself a score between 0% and 100% to indicate where each of your energy cylinders is 'right now'.

   Physical ____ Mental ____ Emotional ____ Spiritual ____

3. **Balancing task and energy**
   Consider the top three tasks or goals that you want to tackle at this time and write them down below. Think about the energy in each cylinder that is required to help you achieve each task to your best standard. You may want to give each energy a certain percentage, like 25%, 50%, 75%, 100%. Alternatively, you could just put a tick next to each cylinder that at the present moment feels sufficient to perform well overall and a cross next to any cylinder that doesn't.

   Task 1_____

   Physical ____ Mental ____ Emotional ____ Spiritual ____

   Task 2_____

   Physical ____ Mental ____ Emotional ____ Spiritual ____

   Task 3_____

   Physical ____ Mental ____ Emotional ____ Spiritual ____

Reflective Questions

- What does each cylinder feel like when it is at 100% for you? Which cylinders are you using most and least? What difference would working on all four cylinders at 100% make to your overall productivity?
- Looking at your cylinders right now, what do the four levels say about your general wellbeing and productivity? Which

11

of your key tasks/goals are well matched to your current energy levels? Are these your high-priority goals? If not, what do you need to do to prepare yourself to tackle your key goals?

- Each cylinder requires specific activities that help replenish its level to your personal 100%. How do you normally replenish your cylinders other than through simply taking time off? What else could you try to do when each cylinder is low?

- If you look backwards in time over a few months or even years, which cylinder do you neglect the most for yourself or people you work or live with? What will help you remember to keep it at a high level?

 ## ASSESS YOUR ENERGY LEVELS: TAKEAWAY LESSONS

Having ample energy for action is key for high-level productivity. When you know what your best looks like and feels like, you have a personal reference point. As you master this exercise, you will be able to assess your energy levels in seconds. This means you can quickly match tasks to your energy levels or focus attention on restoring your energy. If you cannot raise your energy to what is required, consider tackling another task where the demands match your current state, or think about how to adjust the size of your task so it becomes do-able. Either way, you will be most productive by being on top of your energy states.

Some people really benefit from recording their energy levels in a journal over time. You may decide to track your energy each day over a two-week period, or note your energy levels in the morning, at midday and in the evening for a few days. As you bring more awareness and attention to your body, you will develop greater sensitivity and insight about how energy states affect your overall performance and how you can help control them through specific activities. This will allow you to look after yourself well and deliver top-level results on a consistent basis.

3

FIND YOUR ENERGY DRAINS AND ENHANCERS

Where and how you spend time is largely a matter of the constant choices you have to make. These choices reflect your internal values and your changing preferences and needs. What you devote attention to in the present has a powerful impact on your future. Whether it is choosing a specific career path, choosing a partner or picking a restaurant, all our choices contribute to, shape and alter what happens next. The degree to which the choices you make match your values and satisfy your needs determines your everyday fulfilment.

We all have an internal fulfilment sensor which is constantly taking a reading on our activities to let us know how well we are honouring our values. The reading is our sense of happiness and we can get a handle on this through our feelings. When your activities align with your values, you experience high inner energy and a continuing sense of joy no matter how hard you are working or what's going on in your life. When you are largely out of sync with or ignore your values, you experience low energy, resistance and inner conflict. You may feel drained as your internal alarm alerts you to check in. This fulfilment sensor can be a very useful signal for prompting you to take action that will help you restore happiness.

The following Fulfilment Sensor is an excellent exercise to help you identify specific external conditions that either enhance your satisfaction or drain it. It can also help you fine tune activities so that you get more out of them. Awareness of these conditions and effects creates an important external lever of control. Once you identify what drains energy and what adds to it, it is your responsibility to make a conscious decision to either persist with things as they are or change them. Energy drainers and enhancers can be people, tasks, activities, spaces, objects and thoughts. In fact, you may wish to examine each of these broad groups in turn.

This exercise stimulates the creation of explicit knowledge and identification of better alternatives. It also allows a quick mechanism for changing your energy level simply by picking a more constructive option. Remember, your energy is vital to your ability to take action and be at your best. You have a lot of control in terms of what and who you decide to surround yourself with. The results from this exercise tend to remain stable for some time. However, you will benefit from repeating this activity from time to time to ensure you are giving yourself optimal conditions to be at your best.

FULFILMENT SENSOR EXERCISE

1. Pick an area you want to focus on: people in your life or at work, various surroundings, tasks, different jobs/roles you perform, etc.

2. Note down the relative position of each of the above along the following energy continuum. You may wish to do this on a separate piece of paper, in a journal or on your computer.

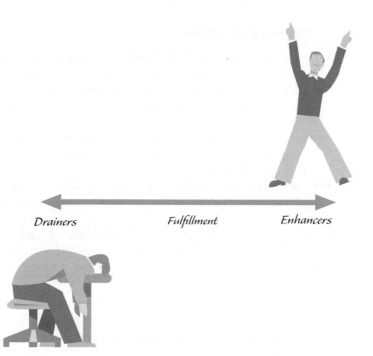

Drainers   Fulfillment   Enhancers

At one end place items that take you away from a feeling of fulfilment, and at the other place those that help create it. If the item feels neutral, place it towards the middle of the line. Note that everything you list has the capacity to shift either up or down, so what's key is how these things affect you right now.

3. Circle your key enhancers and your most severe drainers. You may need to pay attention to how frequently these activities pop up in your life, work or both. If you can increase the frequency or duration of the enhancers or limit/eliminate your drainers in a way that improves your wellbeing, make a note of how you plan to do that and act on it immediately.

Reflective Questions

- On balance are things distributed equally across your sensor? Where are you giving up control too readily or not defining clear boundaries around your own needs in a way that is leaving you drained? What can you do to change this?
- What is the one major change you can make, to either an existing enhancer or drainer, that will most significantly change your fulfilment level?
- What sorts of interactions and/or people help you feel a high degree of fulfilment? Do you have a similar effect on them?
- Can you see specific changes that would meet your existing needs and leave you feeling far more fulfilled? If so, note them down. Don't be afraid to ask for help and create what you want.

 FIND YOUR ENERGY DRAINS AND ENHANCERS: TAKEAWAY LESSONS

Enjoying a sense of fulfilment on a daily basis is great! It allows for the experience of happiness and contentment. How much enjoyment a person derives from each activity will vary at different times in his or her life. The activity need not be easy to be fulfilling. Many entrepreneurs, for example, work very long hours and yet feel a great deal of satisfaction from creating their own business. In fact, many of the most fulfilling tasks connect with a great deal of hard work and sacrifice. Having knowledge of the things that contribute towards a greater sense of fulfilment for you as well as those that don't is a powerful awareness tool. It may give you clues as to why you perform well in some contexts and not in others with relatively high precision. It allows you to control where and how you invest your energy and time to improve your overall satisfaction. Consciously considering what effect each activity, person or change has or can have on your overall fulfilment helps you to make better decisions about how to approach each situation to create the best outcomes and feel great too.

After working through the Fulfilment Sensor you may choose to omit certain activities, behaviours or people entirely because you may not be able to figure out how to turn them into fulfilling or even neutral items. This is how some people decide to quit a job, for example. After some simple analysis they notice that what they do no longer fulfils them at work. Other times you can find better alternatives or limit the frequency or occurrence of specific activities that deplete you. For example, you can consider how to make unfulfilling tasks and jobs more enjoyable. Remember, you are in control of your life and it is up to you to arrange your life in a way that fulfils you, as long as you remain respectful of others. As you increase your awareness, you will soon notice that you can readily identify and create conditions that support your happiness over those that cause you to feel unhappy on a regular basis.

The Fulfilment Sensor is a good exercise to revisit from time to time. If you take notes you can review your decisions, as things can easily slide along the spectrum in either direction. Often people uncover a number of consistent enhancers that tend to remain stable over time. This is a great insight as it provides a powerful resource when needed. One of your chief aims in life is to create conditions that help you do and be your best in the present moment. Perhaps you discover that you need additional help to create the right changes. No problem. There are many inspiring and gifted professionals that can help you create what you want. Don't delay. Even big changes start small. The key is to start!

4

IMPROVE HOW YOU CONNECT WITH OTHERS

Productivity cannot exist without productive relationships. Being able to work well with others is key to your success whether at work, in business or your family life. And yet one of the biggest challenges for many people is to build and maintain relationships that are fruitful, honest, based on trust and mutual respect and which support their success instead of robbing them of energy and motivation. This is especially difficult in the workplace where we don't always choose the people we work with, but may apply equally to your next-door neighbour, your partner or your children.

Having effective relationships across different domains of your life – family, friends, colleagues, business contacts, clients and employees as well as romantic relationships – is a sign of true productivity. Effective interactions begin and remain effective when you pay attention. As you become an active observer of what is happening in the moment, you are able to react to what is, instead of what you want things to be like. It is too easy to get caught in the head games, assumptions, judgements and stories we make up to explain what we think might be going on. This can distract us from focusing on what we really want, which is to have productive and blossoming interactions. Can there really be a magic wand to transform all of your relationships into productive ones? No. However, there is a lot of magic you can do to improve how you interact with the people around you.

The Relationship Magic Wand exercise is based on a simple principle of noticing how you show up in different relationships (those that are productive and those that are less so or not at all) and identifying what is different about *you*. That's right – you. The exercise assumes this because we have no power to change the other person. You can only change your own approach, what you do and say and hope that this improves the result. I have worked with many people who struggled within specific relationships and yet had few problems in many others. On closer inspection, in many instances they ended up creating better outcomes by understanding their own behaviour in more detail. I can assure you that, with time and practice, the Magic Wand will help you improve most of your relationships, so that you touch more people with your magic.

RELATIONSHIP MAGIC WAND EXERCISE

1. Think about two relationships in your life or work at the moment: one hugely productive and one less so or not at all. If you can't think of one right now, do the exercise with a relationship from your past.

2. Starting with the productive relationship, note down a complete description of how you behave(d) in this relationship including what you say (said), what you do (did) and how you act(ed). Be as exhaustive as possible. Pretend you have been asked for a character description for an actor who will play your part. Do not pay attention to the other person or note down how they showed up. Focus entirely on you.

Notes:

3. Now consider the unproductive relationship and note down a complete description of how you behave(d) in this relationship. What do (did) you tend to say? How do (did) you view the other person?

Notes:

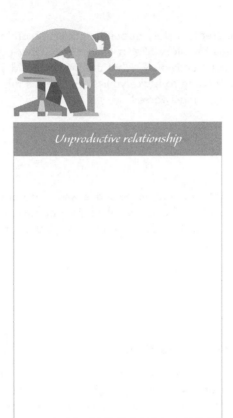

4. What did you bring to each relationship from the start that was the same? Is there anything that you notice that was different between how you were in each example? This may include things like being nervous, anxious, less trusting and so on.

Notes:

5. Did you create a story about the other person in your mind? What was the story like in each case? How does the story affect your behaviour? What assumptions did you make or are you making to make your story true? Is this helping you or making things worse?

Notes:

6. Assuming that the other person is/was good at noticing how you behave(d), what do you think your behaviour would most likely evoke in them? Is it what you wanted or want in this relationship?

Notes:

 Reflective Questions

- What makes you consciously notice for the first time how your relationships are going? What do you need to pay more attention to in all of your relationships so that they become magical?
- What are you most likely to do when things are not working out? What effect would such action(s) normally have? What are you learning about the impact of your behaviour in relationships?
- How would you describe the relationship you have with yourself? Do you treat yourself with admiration and respect? Do you trust your decisions and choices? How does this impact on your relationships with other people?
- What, if anything, do you need to address within yourself in terms of your needs/expectations to ensure the best chance of success for your future interactions with others and for your existing relationships?

IMPROVE HOW YOU CONNECT WITH OTHERS: TAKEAWAY LESSONS

Relationships rarely stay static. They tend to either improve in time or worsen. So whatever trend you notice within each of your key relationships, be mindful of which way things are going. As you complete this exercise, I hope you notice that you have a lot of power to change the outcome of different interactions. You might have also discovered some of your own sensitivities or insecurities that certain interactions may bring out in you and the way that makes you behave. What tends to put your guard up, for example, and what makes you extend a big credit of trust? You might have discovered that you invent a story about each person you interact with. We can't help but do that to some extent.

To ensure the best chance of having successful relationships, it is critical that we do not become attached to our stories, but in fact use questions to check what is, rather than jumping to conclusions. As you might have noticed, the story can have a big impact on your behaviour. Without conscious and proactive questioning of the facts, you can be blinded by your own story. This means that it is easier to take action and interpret events in a way that reinforces your story even when you are actually mistaken. This can be very costly in terms of producing fruitful relationships.

The more you learn about yourself through reflection and analysis of different relationships, the more you will understand what you need and must create for yourself within each interaction to ensure it works for you. I encourage you to really review and understand how you are in your most productive relationships and to use this as a successful compass for all your relationships. So, if you're normally funny, lighthearted, genuine, sincere and helpful, but notice that you're not this way with someone else, then stop and pay attention. Get curious about what the difference might be and how you can return yourself to your best state. This is your magic wand and it's yours to wield.

5

SIMPLIFY UNNECESSARY COMPLEXITY

Complexity can exist within organizations, teams and in one's personal life. A product can be too complex to operate or a brand too difficult to get our heads around to understand its unique selling point. However it shows up, unnecessary complexity makes it hard to get things done at an individual, group or institutional level. It comes about as a result of a difference between what is needed and the process or processes that support the need. In times of frequent change, such gaps arise all the time. Left unchecked, they can undermine results or bring things to a halt. However, once identified, superfluous complexity that has outlived its purpose can easily be eliminated. On a personal level, unnecessary complexity might mean a poorly defined job description, lack of clear goals, no specific responsibilities, poor productivity and time-management processes or just being very disorganized.

Different people's perception of personal productivity varies depending on their self-awareness, life circumstances, life stage, age, culture and the environment. Productivity is strongly linked with time and how we use it. Most people give time a certain value either consciously, by being very aware of what each hour or minute costs, or unconsciously, by noting its passage. Therefore, although how you use time will link to how productive you think you are across all of life's activities, the link is certainly not linear.

Comparisons with other people, also known as 'keeping up with the Joneses', are not terribly helpful. In many cases, such comparisons can be damaging to your confidence, performance and wellbeing. If you compare yourself too favourably, you risk becoming arrogant and complacent. If you compare yourself too unfavourably, you risk cheating yourself out of your true potential, as your energy becomes diverted into paralysis, envy and/or self-doubt. The best comparison, then, seems to be an internal one against your inner energy, your values, dreams, needs and desires.

A high degree of self-awareness, your performance standards and capability are the best measures of how time is spent and what you achieve. As time is a fixed quantity and many activities require significant fractions of the total time you have, your time becomes highly precious, whether you decide to give time to yourself or to others. This means that processes that are overly complex and which steal time away from your most valuable and important activities are costing you a lot more than you realize. In fact, seeing time as a valuable and scarce commodity can quickly help you to simplify your life.

The Simplifier is a great exercise to help identify unnecessary complexities that undermine your performance and results and drop them. I am always amazed by the power of this activity and the number of people who find they have things they can simplify or bin. It highlights the simple fact that most people engage in some activities and processes that waste valuable time either because they no longer need doing or because there is a better and more efficient way of doing them.

THE SIMPLIFIER EXERCISE

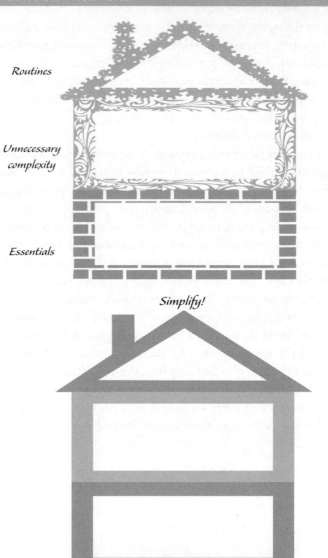

Routines

Unnecessary
complexity

Essentials

Simplify!

1. Make a list of the bare essentials your life or work requires. Aim for the most economic, minimalistic version that satisfies your needs. Your list may include things like: food, shelter, safety, income, accommodation, love, communication devices, etc.

   Notes:

2. Compare this list with your current life and note the extras. Where does the extra complexity come from? For example, it might be information overload, lots of paper, unnecessarily excessive lifestyle, too many gadgets, too much space and/or too much stuff, etc. You may wish to interrogate your existing diary for ideas about the various things you do on a regular basis.

3. Note down existing routines you have for getting things done in a way that saves you time. For example, you might shop online, plan your outfits ahead of time, pay your expenses on a certain day of the month, work from home, use Skype for meetings to limit air flights, etc. If you don't have any routines, note down ideas for routines that would make things easier for you.

   Notes:

4. Examine each area in turn and consider how you might simplify it. What can be binned, outsourced, replaced, decluttered, purged, etc? And what might you need to introduce?

Reflective Questions

- What does your simplified life look like? What is truly essential?
- What external changes/advances increase complexity in your life the most? What is the impact of it on you? What do you need to pay attention to in order to ensure that things remain simple?
- Can you spot any unnecessary complexity in your interactions with others? If so, what can be done about it?
- What are the biggest benefits for you of keeping things simple? What is the impact on others you work with or live with?

SIMPLIFY UNNECESSARY COMPLEXITY: TAKEAWAY LESSONS

Relatively simple and totally effective, the Simplifier should help you identify all sorts of complexities that literally trap you, mess up your thinking, cause you stress and generally rob you of high productivity. Even if you managed to simplify one activity, process or area of your life, you have succeeded! You will feel lighter, re-energized and notice quick improvement in your mental clarity and ability to focus on what's important to you as you eliminate unnecessary distractions.

While simplifying things may take some initial investment, it will save you valuable time in the long run. You may wish to use specific services to help you get organized. If you want to eliminate complexity in your business, you may need to work with an external consultant. External specialists are highly effective because they can remain more objective and deal with processes, activities and items far more dispassionately. They don't have the same attachment to the habits that your unnecessary complexity and disorganization provide for you. Also, they are excellent sources of valuable tips and information about better alternatives. Therefore, the Simplifier is a great activity to be performed on a routine basis, either on your own or with others you work and live with, to help you create better conditions for your success.

6

FIGURE OUT YOUR
KEY PRIORITIES

Nothing comes close to the heart of general productivity like doing the things you really want to do, doing them efficiently and getting the desired results. However, as time passes, we often accumulate activities that, while not necessarily ones we can drop, certainly don't seem to attract high-level enthusiasm, commitment or drive.

In today's busy world, many people are doing more and more tasks and end up feeling worn out, tired and dissatisfied. They might feel overcommitted or caught in a frenzy of doing things while not knowing exactly why. Some people opt for doing things that are easy when what they really want to do is something far more ambitious. This might take the form of an unfulfilling job, or relatively safe projects or a 'good enough' relationship. Spending time on safe but not highly rewarding activities might be a good strategy during uncertainty. However, longer periods of it tend to result in lower morale, dissatisfaction and that infamous feeling of boredom! If protracted, this state can end up causing high levels of stress and depression, and can generally lower one's health and sense of fulfilment.

The Diamonds, Gold and Lead exercise is good for identifying what's really important, what you are currently doing and what is and is not a good time investment. It will help you pinpoint activities that deserve more of your attention as well as raise your awareness about others that you might be outgrowing or have indeed long outgrown. Some of these tasks might still need to be done and the exercise will stimulate you to think about how to achieve them in a better way. Diamonds, Gold and Lead will provide you with greater clarity about what you're doing at the moment and what you need to change, whether for career management, general work satisfaction or even arranging your daily or weekly work schedule for high-level productivity by mixing up work as you would a well-balanced meal.

The exercise sorts all activities into five areas:

1. **Diamonds:** activities that are truly special and unique, things that help you develop and grow and which improve your life massively.
2. **Rough diamonds:** activities that will turn into diamonds down the line and which are appearing on the horizon.
3. **Gold:** activities that are worthwhile because they contribute steadily to your resources, your worth and your stability.
4. **False gold:** activities that appear to be gold but end up as energy sinkers and time drainers, often disappointing and causing hurt.
5. **Lead:** activities that take time but which no longer contribute positively towards your present situation or your future.

Every activity at a specific point in time, in one's career or life stage, can be assigned to one of these five areas.

One of the key benefits of this highly beloved activity is that, once assigned, you will automatically adjust your attention and time so that you concentrate on high-level activities and begin to prioritize work easily in accordance with its position. I have found this exercise hugely fruitful when working with individuals, groups and even entire organizations. In fast-changing times, it is imperative that you do not waste valuable time on activities that are no longer precious and keep your competitive edge by exploring and mining your figurative diamonds.

DIAMONDS, GOLD AND LEAD EXERCISE

1. Think about all the key activities you engage with currently at work and/or in your life. This may include specific projects, relationships, activities, interests, groups, etc.

2. Assign each activity to one of these five areas: real diamonds, rough diamonds, gold, false gold and lead. You may want to take each area in turn or simply outline all in one go.

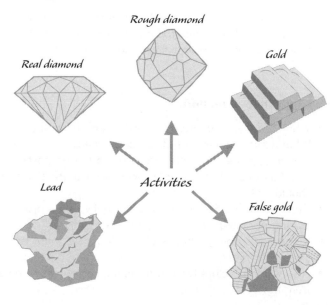

Notes:

3. Return to this exercise at regular intervals to help you save valuable time, keep your focus on high-level activities and stay in control of what you decide to do and why.

 Reflective Questions

- What is/are your diamond/diamonds at this time?
- What do you generally notice about where your effort and time goes at the moment? Where do you focus most of your attention and where do you focus none of it? Is this as it should be?
- Can you find activities that are currently in the process of shifting positions? Which way are they shifting?
- If you keep doing what you're doing now, what are the likely outcomes?
- How will this picture look in a month, six months or a year from now?

FIGURE OUT YOUR KEY PRIORITIES: TAKEAWAY LESSONS

What people often observe when doing this exercise is that things have a way of moving around and they are not terribly aware of this. For example, something that might have been gold at one point in time may stay gold, transform into a diamond or turn into lead. Equally, things that might have appeared to be lead can sometimes turn out to be rough diamonds. Imagine a network of casual contacts. One day, one of these people may turn out to be the critical link or support you need, or a very good friend. A product your company was developing as a sideline may become your unique selling point. Similarly, a hobby can sometimes feel like false gold only to turn into a lucrative business venture.

Many people spend disproportionate amounts of time working up false gold and lead instead of rough diamonds, not because they choose to do this but because they have forgotten to stop and examine what they are doing. With more and more things to do it is easy to get lost in the activities and end up losing focus on the most valuable ones. The same holds true for teams and organizations. While very simple, this exercise can help you pinpoint key information in a short amount of time with high precision.

7

OVERCOME YOUR PROCRASTINATION WITH ACTION

Procrastination is a true monster that takes away confidence and ultimately undermines self-worth. It also saps vital energy. Every time you delay something, you add imaginary weight onto your shoulders while the item joins the long queue of to-do items: a burden of a promise you need to fulfil. Over time this burden grows and grows and your self-worth shrinks in its shadow. You drag along a big suitcase of things you can't seem to get around to but which you nonetheless want to, or think you need to, get done *soon*.

There are times when procrastinating is useful. For example, when you require more information or are unclear about what to do. In each case, procrastination is, in fact, a real signal for taking specific action such as seeking advice or gathering further information.

Perpetual procrastination on tasks that require immediate attention, such as work, bills, travel arrangements, booking fun activities, working out logistics for your holiday or even tackling that CV for a better job, kills productivity. Such actions are important yet can be easy to postpone. Tackling them head on means you are taking consistent action without having to be pushed by impending deadlines or final notices. As a result, you're being highly productive because you're taking ownership of your decisions and actions.

Taking action on the things you procrastinate on allows you to develop trust in yourself. No one will trust you enough unless you trust yourself first. Be accountable, professional and trustworthy.

The Procrastinator Buster is a muscle-building exercise. The goal of it is simply to build the necessary resilience to overcome procrastination and take action. I do this exercise with individual clients to help them discover their power of resolve and self-integrity. Your goal is to tackle only one task and get yourself into the discipline of starting. Most people can get themselves to do things at the last minute under the pressure of deadlines. This is different. By mastering your own procrastinator you are learning to take action in the moment. This is vital to creating impactful results and getting things done. You do not need a reason other than you deciding to take action. Regular practice here will save you lots of last-minute rushes and will significantly increase your sense of balance and control.

PROCRASTINATOR BUSTER EXERCISE

1. Take a deep breath. Good. Now take another one. And another. Exhale slowly each time. Allow your body to feel the benefit of your breath and the power that is growing inside you. Yes, you! You are about to kick your procrastinator out. You will send it flying spectacularly into the sky, and as you do it you will feel the energy, confidence, lightness and motivation that remain in its place – the source of your productivity to accomplish whatever you need to.

2. Now, write down a list of things you have been putting off. This list should include items that:
   (i)   when accomplished, will leave you better off than you are at the moment, i.e. doing each one will move you ahead in some real way;

(ii) are things you need to do eventually or which you should have done by now and which only weigh you down;

(iii) can be done in roughly the same time it takes to contemplate doing them and letting the procrastinator take over;

(iv) you just can't seem to get yourself to do even though you would laugh at someone else if they told you about it.

Notes:

3. Having assembled your procrastination list, look at each item in turn and note down the exact reason why you're not getting on with the task. Many people do this step on a computer as they often keep a long to-do list of tasks they need to complete but procrastinate on.

Your reasons might be similar to these examples:

(i) this is not very important in the scheme of things;

(ii) I don't know how to get started;

(iii) I really hate this task;

(iv) it would be nice to get it done but I don't feel like doing it;

(v) I'm scared, nervous, confused, etc.

4. Having named the real reasons you're procrastinating, go through your list again and cross out all the items that you noted are not important right now. If they become important later, they will resurface on their own as real priorities.

5. Then pick one item from the remaining list where you feel you can make immediate and worthwhile progress. It's your turn to bust procrastination.

What am I putting off?	Why?	My action knowing this.

Procrastination

Self-worth / self-belief

Reflective Questions

- Looking at your original list, what do you tend to procrastinate on and why? What stops you from taking action? What are you missing or lacking in each case?
- How do you feel after tackling your procrastination? What are you learning about yourself through this exercise?
- What assumptions do you tend to make when you procrastinate about the task, the time it will take or the outcome? Are these helpful?

 OVERCOME YOUR PROCRASTINATION WITH ACTION: TAKEAWAY LESSONS

Doing this exercise will help you to realize that what you tend to procrastinate on are often actions that are relatively small and may not take very long once you start, but which often appear far larger. This is normal. As you procrastinate, the thoughts about doing the actions grow. The actions balloon in size without the real work increasing at all. The Procrastinator Buster helps you focus on the real action steps required to get the job done. Sometimes the action involves drawing a line in the sand and eliminating the tasks, delegating the work to others or breaking it down into work you can crack on with right away. As you take purposeful action you become productive again and you beat the procrastinator within you.

Being able to take action is key to success. And I know you will feel amazing every time you switch from vague, indefinite delays and take control of what you create. With time, you will build a muscle without even thinking about the exercise – but you also need to be patient. Eventually, your in-tray will get smaller, your inbox will be empty at the end of the day and you will actually have time to ask those important questions such as *What else do I really fancy doing?* You will sleep better and smile more. Now that's productivity in its best form.

8

CREATE A 'FEEL GOOD' STATE

People tend to do their best work and achieve impressive results when they are feeling good. A positive mindset makes a big difference in how we approach life, the company we attract and our overall productivity. Merged with clear focus and determination to take action, a positive mindset is a key determinant of success.

Can a mindset really cause such a massive shift you wonder? Yes it can. People with a more negative attitude give up sooner and expect things to be difficult. Faced with setbacks, they require far greater resilience and motivation to keep going while part of their mind is constantly saying they won't make it. People with a positive mindset approach a task positively, believing they can make it and focus their energy on thinking about the 'how'.

The mental state you're in at any given moment is a binary choice. When you think positive thoughts you engage specific neural pathways. When you think negative thoughts you amplify negative emotions. The mindset you adopt is your choice! Everyone can develop the skills of thinking positive thoughts. The more you experience positive emotions, the easier it is to keep them.

The Feel Good Pill exercise is based on the idea that feel good states can be elicited on demand with practice using specific triggers or by choosing what you pay attention to in any given moment. This, in turn, means that you can literally make yourself feel better and keep yourself in a more productive state. As you complete this exercise you will discover and help strengthen your own feel good factors so that you can call on them when you need to feel great.

1. Think about a time when you were happiest or when you felt simply unstoppable – a moment when you were taking action and you felt absolutely fantastic! Relive the moment in full Technicolor. Close your eyes to help you visualize it. If you can think of more than one scenario, examine each one in turn and pick the strongest. This is your peak moment.

2. Working with your peak scenario that makes you feel great, tune into the sounds, the people around you and your surroundings. Notice how your body feels, how you stand or sit and how the feeling of massive power, excitement, energy,

happiness or whatever it is that makes you feel great soars within you.

3. Practise tuning back into the same moment or situation, so that a wide smile appears on your face and you literally begin to feel good as soon as you recreate it in your mind. It might be someone's face that makes you smile, or a voice that calms you or a piece of clothing that makes you feel fabulous. It might be the feeling of sand beneath your feet or the warmth of the sun on your cheeks on a beautiful day. Your goal is to be able to get to a point where, without fail, you can create your feel good pill.

 Reflective Questions

- What generally makes you feel good? Be as specific and descriptive as possible.
- What do you need to do to feel that way if you want to now? Close your eyes and take yourself back to these moments as if you were watching a short film. Run it through a few times until you begin to feel the same feelings again. Then run it a few more times.
- Feeling positive like this, what are some of the things you feel you're able to do? Circle any that you really wish you'd got started with already.
- Given what you have discovered about your feel good moments, what are some possible next ones? What will you do to make them happen?

 ## CREATE A 'FEEL GOOD' STATE: TAKEAWAY LESSONS

Powerful experiences (both positive and negative) evoke a strong emotional response. These emotions affect feelings, thought patterns and behaviour. If you completed this exercise correctly, you will now have sound knowledge about what makes you feel good and what factors help put you into a positive state. The trigger can be anything. Only you need to know what it is; it could be the feeling of your favourite outfit, for example. There's a reason why many confidence coaches encourage their clients to buy an expensive suit or dress. When you look impressive, your confidence grows too and this will change your behaviour. Also, by spending a special sum on you, you are, in fact, telling yourself that you matter, which will raise your sense of self-worth.

When you think positive thoughts, you tend to act from a more optimistic place and notice more possibilities in the world around you. Thus, having a positive state of mind has the potential to make you more resourceful. A big fraction of happiness is about being in control: experiencing life on your terms. Everyone experiences moments when this is true; times when you feel inspired, great or unstoppable.

The Feel Good Pill helps you draw on the power of your mind and apply it to control how you feel. You can recreate positive feelings when you want to by using triggers from your memories, experiences or surroundings. You have a choice about how you feel in any instant. You can be miserable, down on your luck, sad or feel left out. Or, you can choose to feel happy, motivated and on top of the world. What the mind pays attention to or imagines, the body turns into action. Using past experiences works well because they are real. However, your mind is a very powerful simulator as well. Using guided visualization with the assistance of a qualified professional, you can *imagine* specific situations that will make you feel good too. Using the method in this exercise, you ought to be able to find triggers and generate a number of specialized pills to help you smile, relax, focus, pay attention or anything else you may find useful. I hope you will get creative and experiment with this exercise.

SECTION TWO

TO DO: GET TO KNOW SELF

I don't know about you but there are times when I do something and wonder later on what exactly it was that drove me to do it. It wasn't until I began to reflect on what I valued and needed in life that some of these seemingly irrational choices, as well as seemingly inexplicable actions, including procrastination, began not just to make pretty good sense but to be outright common sense. I have noticed the same thing when working as a thinking partner with some of the most clever and visionary people in the world. Our brains are far smarter than we realize and they aim to help us be at our best. For example, for a period of a year I walked barefoot in my home. It wasn't until a few months later that I realized that my body was naturally finding a way to help me feel grounded through physical contact with the earth. When stability and a sense of control returned, my need to walk barefoot went away.

The experience got me curious. Understanding some of the drivers for the patterns and habits I developed over the years has been an eye opener and a great lever for improving the productivity of my clients and myself. Exercises in this section are designed to help you get to know yourself at a deeper level. This will help you move towards what you want with authenticity and alignment with your own style and nature.

9

EXAMINE WHAT'S IMPORTANT FOR YOU NOW

Broadly speaking, our time as adults tends to be divided among three main categories: work, play (fun, reactivation) and relationships. True productivity means getting the results we want across all three areas. Activities within the work area include careers, jobs, chores and other key life responsibilities such as parenthood. Playtime is the time spent on hobbies, interests and other fun activities – things that bring one pleasure. Relationship time is the time spent with others and the time spent with ourselves.

The three areas overlap with each other – for example, to some people, work brings meaningful friendship and opportunities to play. When such overlap occurs you feel absorbed in the moment and can derive maximum pleasure from the experience. Such absorbance is often called being in the 'flow' or 'zone'. More often than not though, you may find that you are forced to choose between time spent at work, at play or on your relationships. For example, you might need to travel for work and be away from your family. The world of work, however, is changing. Increasingly people choose jobs that deliver fun and monetary rewards. Technology is also making office work significantly more portable.

The actual amount of time you spend in each of the three sectors is closely linked to what you need and desire most. For example, some people value relationships and fun a lot more than the exact manner in which they earn their living (work). Such individuals will often be less concerned with job status, titles or the exact nature of what it is they do.

I once met a young man who worked for an events company. He passed up a number of promotions in order to ensure that he could spend as much time as possible with his girlfriend. His managers could not understand his behaviour but to him, his decision to pass up promotion made perfect sense. He associated promotion with a more rigid work schedule and, because his partner's work was also unpredictable, this, in his mind, would limit the amount of time he could spend with her.

There are people who draw massive satisfaction from work – it provides them with the fun factor and, at times, even key relationships from colleagues and work friends. They may willingly sacrifice their free time, weekends and holidays for work. These people may value achievement, work itself, career and success as very important and will find their highest level of personal fulfilment and self-realization in work.

Each person will value the three areas differently. The satisfaction level with the results you achieve in each area reflects the extent to which your needs are met. Since you are responsible for creating your own happiness, it should also tell you a great deal about whether you are being truly productive or not. The order of importance across the three areas you give for yourself will determine how you spend your time and ultimately guide the choices you make. This is especially true when you need to choose between different activities or find motivation to act. It is during such choices that people's natural preferences and values become clearer and where hurdles towards goal realization are easy to spot. Knowledge of self and awareness about which activities you prefer and enjoy creates the certainty required for making choices or finding satisfactory alternatives.

The Work, Play, Relationship Juice exercise is a very useful activity to help establish the overall priority of these areas in your life, to identify what's key within each area in terms of desired results and to evaluate your productivity. This exercise should also be very effective at helping you to identify your absolute 'musts' versus your wish list. Both the overall priority you give to each area and the activities within them will change over time. Therefore, this is a great activity to revisit when you want to check how you're doing against what you really want out of life.

WORK, PLAY, RELATIONSHIP JUICE EXERCISE

1. Pick your juice mix. Take a moment now to note down your own preference for the three areas and their relative importance in your life at this point in time. People say you have to make sacrifices. I disagree. When you know yourself and what you want and you stay true to that, you find ways to balance the juice appropriately.

   Notes:

2. Note down what activities would make up each of the three
    main ingredients to make your juice taste super sweet.

    WORK:

    PLAY:

    RELATIONSHIPS:

3. Have a look at each ingredient and note those you have right
    now versus those still missing. If there are extra ingredients
    – things you don't have in your life right now but would like
    to have – note them down. These could be friendships, visit-
    ing specific places in the world, work accomplishments, etc.
    For each one, note down a rough timeline about when you
    would like to have them in your juice: in a few months, next
    year or two to three years from now.

    Notes:

4. What's going on with your ingredients at the moment? Are
    they what you want to have? Is one area sweeter (closer to
    your ideal) than the others? What did you have to do to make
    it so?

    Notes:

5. Write down what your preferred juice mix looks like. What's
    definitely in? If you can pinpoint the exact proportions, that's
    even better.

    Notes:

6. Look back in time to three, five or even ten years ago and note down what your juice looked like back then. If there's a change between what you had back then and what you have now, is it a positive shift? Write down any specific actions or decisions you made that allowed for this.

Notes:

7. Draw or note down what you would like your life juice to look like in the future.

Relationships   Play   Work

 Reflective Questions

- Is the way you approach decisions about how you spend time consistent with the juice you want to drink? If not, what adjustments do you need to make with your decisions? What will help you do that?
- What are the absolute musts within your ingredients? How can you ensure these are present?

- What do you need to pay more attention to, if anything, given what you have discovered? How will you ensure you do that?
- What assumptions, if any, are you making about your juice and are they based on facts?

 ## EXAMINE WHAT'S IMPORTANT FOR YOU NOW: TAKEAWAY LESSONS

Many people, especially in business, will have you believe that to succeed you have to make sacrifices. I disagree. When you know yourself and what you want and you stay true to that, you find ways to balance your juice appropriately. People who make 'sacrifices' do so because they are too scared of creating an amazing life for fear of losing it, not too clear about what fulfilment looks like or have not mastered true productivity. They are going to find that life presents them with many regrets at some stage and it may be too late to change that. It can be easy to lose yourself in work or in a relationship or in a play juice. However, without the correct balance that will fulfil all of your needs, this is a risky strategy for success, especially when things do not go according to plan.

As a coach, I always caution my clients about relying too much on one sort of juice in their life. I hope that working through this exercise has helped you get in touch with all of your needs and priorities so that you can make sound decisions; that it has given you insight about what you most value and what you must have in your life for it to be hugely satisfying. I also hope that developing greater knowledge about yourself helps you make effective relationships with other people whose juice preference might be completely different to yours. This is important for building romantic as well as professional relationships and will save you valuable time and disappointment. Always remember, happiness is found in the moment and not *some fine day*. Don't be scared to claim yours.

10

FIND YOUR KEY VALUES FROM SEEMINGLY RANDOM THINGS

While your preferences can change with circumstances and time, your values tend to stay pretty constant. A particular activity that is a good use of time now might be less preferred in five or ten years' time or even in a couple of weeks. The activities and people you devote time to in the present might lose their importance at a later time point. Activities, interests and relationships can taper off to make way for others to flourish in their place. This is a very natural cycle that allows us to match our changing preferences and needs – and remain productive.

The more you know yourself, the more comfortable you can be about who you are and the easier it becomes to honour and meet your own needs in life. That is the hallmark of healthy individual assertiveness. It is only through understanding, respecting and loving yourself that you can give your best to others. Often this happens as you get older and get to know yourself better. The process of aging helps us appreciate the precious nature of time. But there is no need to wait. The past is gone and the future is made by what you choose to do today.

Values are the master forces that steer you in decisions. What can, at times, feel completely irrational makes perfect sense when you uncover what you truly value, because we can't help but be attracted to what we think is important. Your values make up an inner navigational tool to help you to make decisions that bring your values to life. Values give you standards. When your values are ignored for too long, you may begin to feel unhappy. Fortunately values are written into everything you do. With a bit of careful analysis, like an inspector looking at footprints, you can begin to uncover what you truly value.

The Value Footprints exercise that follows will help pinpoint many of your key values. Gaining insight and knowledge about the values that underpin what we do and prefer not only develops high levels of self-awareness but also allows us to honour our values in action. Your best productivity can only exist on your terms as you live and work in alignment with who you are. Applying the knowledge you gather in this exercise will help you to combine activities creatively in a way that will maximize your fulfilment and happiness on a regular basis.

VALUE FOOTPRINTS EXERCISE

1. Note down between five and seven specific activities, objects, symbols, people and surroundings that you really like. You can do more if you wish. It could be a café you visit regularly, a person you met or someone you've known for some time, an old or new film you saw, your favourite objects, etc.

Activities	Objects	Symbols/ Brands	People	Surroundings

2. Now write down a list of descriptors for each of the things you picked above. For example, you may take your favourite room and say it is: cosy, clean and peaceful.

Notes:

3. When you're done, have a look at the various characteristics and note down those that repeat; these represent things you value.

4. Think about any activities, objects, symbols, people or surroundings that you truly can't stand. What specific values do these items step on? Add them to your values list.

5. On a scale of 0 (not at all) to 10 (100%), to what extent do you currently meet each one of the values you captured? What might you want to do to incorporate your values more in your life and work where this is not currently the case?

Notes:

 Reflective Questions

- To what extent are you consciously aware of the value footprints when you meet new people or explore a new venue?
- Do values influence to what or to whom you pay attention?
- What does the exercise reveal to you about your needs at the moment? You may wish to make a list of needs based on what you discovered. How have they changed or grown?
- If you look at your life, close relationships, work, general lifestyle and your romantic partner, in turn, notice the alignment between the values you uncovered and what you would like ideally to have in each area to be happy.
- How did your values come about? What do they offer you?

FIND YOUR KEY VALUES FROM SEEMINGLY RANDOM THINGS: TAKEAWAY LESSONS

You may not entirely like it, but if you did this exercise correctly you will have found many of the key things you value in life, relationships, places and so on. As your values remain relatively stable over time, if your current work and life neglect them or go against them, you will probably suffer. You may not know why you're suffering. Hopefully, though, as you begin to build awareness about who you are and what's really important to you, you will make choices that help create the necessary conditions for your happiness and success. People who are able to arrange their life in agreement with their values tend to feel more content and satisfied. When there's a misalignment between the two, you may experience frustration, dissatisfaction or feel like something is not quite right.

By looking at Value Footprints you might have also discovered a few of your specific needs. Needs are less permanent than values and change over time. Having your needs met is important before you can let them go. I hope that the exercise will leave you curious and able to learn about yourself using many seemingly random things in your life and environment. In fact, they are not as random as you think, especially when you like them. The more you learn about yourself, the more confident you will become. Grounding yourself in knowledge about who you are will help you make productive choices.

11

DISCOVER YOUR NEEDS AND DESIRES

Just like a physical compass is used for navigation, we each have an inner compass made up of values that motivate us to take action. We also have needs that dictate what we choose to pursue or what attracts us. Some people always move away from things. Their compass is good at detecting what they don't like and they use that information to motivate them and help propel them in another direction. Others move towards things they want. Many people exist in *drift* mode. They are steered away and towards people and activities without taking proactive decisions or they respond to what they need at any given time. They allow external factors to influence their choices like a puppet. It is important to be aware of what you need so that you can work to meet your needs in an elegant way as opposed to getting tempted to meet your needs through actions that may actually hurt you.

The Puppet Strings exercise is a good activity to help develop awareness of your needs and desires. It requires you to systematically identify your needs and desires in key areas of your life: daily life, your relationships, work, your health and your romantic partner. It can also be applied to what you need from a certain project, your pet and so on.

PUPPET STRINGS EXERCISE

1. List what you feel/think you need in each of the areas below. You may find the listed examples useful to prompt your thinking.

Life – (great deal of flexibility, financial security, great romantic partner, home/apartment I love, pleasant and connected local community, good relationships, access to people with ideas, countryside/city balance, having a garden, having an interesting view out of the windows, spirituality, etc.)

Notes:

Relationships – (meaningful and good friendships, having one or more best friends, being connected to people from my childhood, intelligent colleagues, good neighbours, family without strife, boss or business partner(s) I respect and value, etc.)

Notes:

Work – (chance to make a massive difference, challenging projects, opportunity for continuous learning, good pay/ rewards, nice office, flexibility to work from home, personal assistant, leading a team, creating jobs, creative team, fun working culture, etc.)

Notes:

Health/wellbeing – (feeling full of energy each day, being able to run 5 km on a daily basis, going to one spiritual retreat every six months, having time for a slow breakfast, etc.)

Notes:

Romantic partner – (attractive, intelligent, ambitious, kind, generous, loving, romantic, entrepreneurial, spontaneous, fun, etc.)

Notes:

If there's another major category you wish to add, please do so.

Notes:

2. Put your list away for a few days in a safe place and make a new list with the same main headings. In a few days, fill out your new list from scratch and save it. Repeat this step at least three times, leaving a few days between each time so that your mind works on a blank canvas instead of your memory.

3. When you have three or four lists, read through them. Notice the words/themes that consistently pop up for each section. Make a fresh list of headings and note the most frequently appearing words or characteristics. You have just discovered what you need and want right now.

4. Think about your needs as puppet strings and you as a puppet. How do your needs and desires influence your behaviour? You may want to think about how they affect you at work, at home, with your friends, clients, etc.

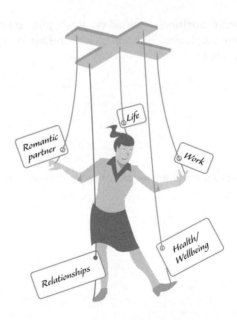

5. Note down how you meet each need at the moment. Are your methods conducive to your overall wellbeing? If not, what are some alternative ways you could meet your needs in a more elegant way?

Notes:

 Reflective Questions

- What is the key priority for you at this point within the five areas? Which needs are strongest and which are weakest?
- What is most important for you in each area? Do your actions and decisions reflect that?
- Are you communicating your needs to your existing or potential partner or assuming they can read your mind?
- Suppose all your needs were met, what do you think you would need then?

 DISCOVER YOUR NEEDS AND DESIRES:
TAKEAWAY LESSONS

In my work with people I have discovered that, whether they know it or not, people are continuously moving towards a place where they can meet their needs and values. Taking the time to understand in detail what your desired life looks like and giving yourself permission to tune into your inner wisdom and greatness to learn about it, is a key first step in bringing this life into existence. Such insight gives your brain a template of what you want, which it can then begin to create through purposeful and effective action. Where I've seen people do this, I have witnessed their sense of satisfaction increase tremendously. When you seek and work on what you truly want, you will be happy in your quest, discover immense inner strength and you will be secure in what you need to realize it. However, when it comes to needs, sometimes the seductive short-term satisfier may not, in fact, be the best choice; for example, drinking to drown grief or quitting a job to satisfy your need to win the argument.

I hope this exercise helps you to discover your needs and assess whether they drive you to take productive actions. When needs are not articulated or met for a long time, people tend to feel dissatisfied and will act out. This can cause disappointment and break up promising relationships. When you lack insight into how you work and what drives you, you can't take responsibility for how you show up and the results you create. Nor can you communicate clearly what you need for others to be able to understand you and help you. This means you are more likely to repeat unconscious patterns of behaviour and get the same poor outcomes even when you change circumstances.

Being able to understand, communicate and assert your needs is a sign of true maturity. It is your responsibility to meet your needs and make yourself happy in a healthy and self-respecting way. No one else can do that for you. And when you do meet your own needs elegantly, you will find yourself in a wonderful place where you can share your happiness with others in a lovely way.

12

USE PAST FAILURES TO BUILD RESILIENCE AND STRENGTH

We are a sum of all our experiences – those we remember fondly and those we wish to forget. Often our learning is greatest in situations that might, at the time, have felt overwhelming or impossible to deal with. There may be aspects of yourself that you find problematic or downright unacceptable. Yet it is those same characteristics that give you your uniqueness and significance. There are also times when certain experiences may be too painful or disappointing and you try to push them away as a way of protecting yourself. However, if you choose to ignore these situations completely and pretend they do not exist, they will become your broken china – the stuff you clear away from view but instead of properly disposing of it, you chuck it into a cupboard you just don't open very often.

If you constantly deny certain aspects of yourself or shut off your past experiences, hoping to forget them without extracting learning from them, you risk leaving integral parts of yourself behind. You also miss out on the learning and growth that such experiences and life have offered you. This is often why people tend to repeat the same mistakes in careers or relationships or fail repeatedly in some task.

The reason for this is that, more often than not, when experiences overwhelm us and we can't deal with them productively, we are either missing specific skills or knowledge. It is only by making mistakes and reflecting on them that we learn what we need to know in order to do better next time. True productivity means you become a humble and eager student of life. Appropriate integration of everything that has happened to you and where you have played a role in creating it allows you to stay centred and to own who you are. This knowledge, acceptance and constant willingness to learn and grow builds authenticity, which is fundamental in effective leadership and building productive, long-lasting relationships. It should help you to admit that, even with the best intentions, you are likely to make mistakes. As you integrate, own and develop an ever-better version of yourself, you no longer have to pretend to be what you're not. You can be who you really are and be proud of it.

The Broken China exercise is useful in coming to terms with past experiences that have not worked out as you wished and in healing them so that they don't rob you of your confidence or limit your opportunities. We always have a role in each situation. When something appears really broken it can be easy to sweep it all under a carpet or forget about it. The trouble with that is that you miss out on good learning points that can help you become more resilient and effective in the future. Refusal to examine the situation and learn also sends an unconscious message to your brain, telling it you can't cope. This message can shrink your world and undermine your self-belief.

All experiences and relationships, however they work out, offer us gifts. Being able to integrate them into your life is a sign of maturity and respect for yourself and for the other person. Your goal in this exercise is a courageous one. You are invited to examine past events and relationships that have not worked out as you would wish, to help you build a more balanced perspective about what you did well and what you might still need to learn. Integration is a great exercise to help life be your learning school. Deepening your self-awareness will help you pinpoint areas where you need to expand what is in your comfort zone. Learning to integrate unsatisfactory experiences effectively will broaden your ability to deal with difficult situations. You will not only save yourself valuable time but, importantly, improve the results you achieve with what you learn.

BROKEN CHINA EXERCISE

1. Think about all the key events in your life so far that have not worked out as you would like. It doesn't matter whether you think/feel these were not your fault at all, but remember to leave nothing behind unless it is hugely traumatic and you feel unable to cope with it. You may wish to do this exercise in three rounds:
   (i) projects;
   (ii) relationships;

(iii) aspects of yourself that you might not like to admit to or feel embarrassed by.

Projects	Relationships	Aspects of yourself
Examples: the job/promotion I didn't get; the business that didn't get off the ground; the project that failed to deliver the intended results, that specific client; etc.	Examples: father; partner; ex partner; girlfriend; neighbour; colleague; boss; etc.	Examples: my shyness; being gay; having no formal education; being boring; feeling stupid; being unattractive; not being able to write well; etc.

2. First take a deep breath of pride. By listing some or all of your difficult experiences, you have taken a massive step towards becoming a much stronger person. That's tremendous. You may wish to stop here for a break or, if you feel ready to continue, follow on with the steps below.

3. Take each example in turn and note down in one sentence what each piece of your broken china is really about. It could be a difference of opinion, a disagreement, a difference in values, a misunderstanding, poor communication, etc. What did you need/want that you didn't get? What did others want?

Notes:

4. What did you do at the time that helped undermine the situation? What did you pay attention to most and what did you ignore that could have been important only you couldn't see it at the time?

Notes:

5. What do you know or are able to do now that you were not able to do in each situation at that time? What were you missing then? What have you learned?

Notes:

6. When you finish considering all the broken china situations/relationships you might have had, note down which of the three areas, if any, collected the most breakages. Note down some ideas about what you can do to develop more skills in this area.

Notes:

Reflective Questions

- As you review the situations from those that happened a long time ago to those that are more recent, what is new that you're learning in each case and what mistakes do you tend to repeat?
- What insights and/or learning points can you extract from these examples about what you struggle with or still find difficult? How can you begin to address this to improve your effectiveness in the future?
- Is there anything that is causing you specific regret? What is the regret about? What will help you let it go or heal it?
- What are you able to accept and integrate into your life in terms of your responsibility in each situation as a result of completing the exercise and what can you leave behind as not yours?

 USE PAST FAILURES TO BUILD RESILIENCE AND STRENGTH: TAKEAWAY LESSONS

The longer we are alive, the easier it can be to accumulate a list of people we fell out with or projects that didn't pan out. We can lose our true selves underneath all the expectations, roles and masks we use to navigate through life. But this doesn't have to, and shouldn't, be the case, especially if you aim to be truly productive.

Some people are embarrassed about where they come from, their socioeconomic status, their level of education or their parents. Some people have a list of relationships that failed or jobs that never worked out or a string of employees that left them not the company. Other people have no such list or one containing only a few items. The difference between the two groups of people is that while one learns and matures, the other continues in denial.

Productivity is about continuous integration and learning, so that next time is always better than the last. I hope that, however difficult or easy this exercise was for you, you walk away from it equipped with at least one critical new insight about yourself. That it gives you ideas or pinpoints specific areas where you can grow and develop your knowledge or skills so that your life and opportunities continuously expand for you; that you learn what was, and perhaps still is, important to you. This might be love, success, freedom, acceptance, fun or many other things. By doing the exercise well, you might have discovered what has kept you in failure for too long and what you must learn to do to move on from it in a healthy way.

Expanding options and choices is an indicator of a truly productive person's life. Don't be afraid to ask for help if needed. There are many professionals that can work with you to help you extract key learning, heal and really step into owning yourself in your totality. You owe it to yourself to eliminate any and all barriers to your best self and to getting what you want in life.

13
CLARIFY YOUR GOALS

We are always taking ourselves towards something. At times, this might represent an explicit and carefully chosen goal; at other times, the direction is less clear and emergent because we are attracted to or repelled from something in an unconscious way. One of the best ways to stay productive is to have clear goals in the form of specific steps or outcomes.

The Goal Highlighter is a useful exercise to bring clarity into what is happening right now and the conscious and unconscious forces that are taking you forward. It helps you map what you want, where this is clear, and to systematically identify specific smaller goals that will support you in that direction. Highlighting your goals builds conscious awareness about areas where you are productive and areas where you are stalling. It will also help you to evaluate how productive your actions are against your desired outcomes, so that you can make any necessary adjustments and ensure success.

GOAL HIGHLIGHTER EXERCISE

1. Write down everything you want at the moment in your life, work, career, home, romantic relationship, etc. For each goal, note down the likely timeframe when you think you can achieve it. An example is shown here:

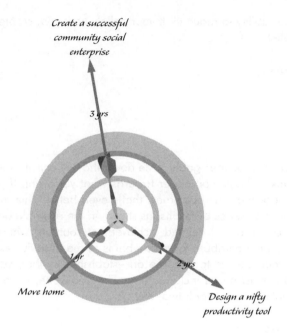

Notes:

2. Note down your main thoughts about each of your goals. Are they useful in terms of helping to motivate you to work towards it or do they make you doubt your goal or your ability to reach it? If your beliefs limit you, create a new belief.

Notes:

3. For each of your goals, note down the key activities that you think will take you closer towards what you want. If you can phrase them as outcomes, that's even better. This might be a logical series of results, as shown in the example below, or a collection of related achievements/outputs where each helps to contribute towards what is at the end. For example, if your goal is to become an established author, your outcomes list might include things like book one, an article, a public lecture, book two, etc.

Notes:

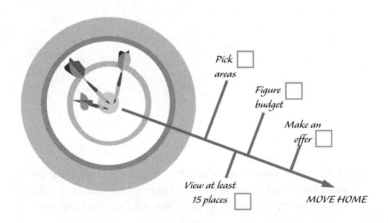

4. Looking at your clear end goals, note down what your life will look like when you achieve them, as it is very likely that you will. Do you like what you see? If so, get going on making some of the outcomes a reality. Take action!

Notes:

5. When you achieve one of the outcomes, tick it off and get going on another. Tackle what you seem ready for, what your life offers you, and work along all dimensions so that you are advancing all of your goals.

6. Periodically review your end goals and timelines to make sure that the effort you're making still resonates with what you want.

 Reflective Questions

- What do your end goals offer you? What do you find motivating about them? What pulls/compels you to take the actions you are taking towards them?
- What needs are your current actions satisfying? Are there other ways in which you can meet these needs that would be better for you?
- Are there any goals that you might have had before that you have had to leave behind or compromise on? Do these decisions feel right to you now and if not what can you do to make a positive change?
- How might you sabotage your goals? What can you put in place to prevent this?

CLARIFY YOUR GOALS: TAKEAWAY LESSONS

The Goal Highlighter is a truly useful way to capture all your goals and track your progress in a way that will help you always to take action in line with the goals you have. Sometimes people act without really considering how this relates to what they want. At times these actions can, on closer inspection, appear to be in direct conflict with what is desired. For example, you might be fighting with someone you care about when, in fact, what you really want is to love him or her. Or you may wish to quit a particular job and yet you keep on volunteering for projects that make it hard to quit. The Goal Highlighter helps you spell out what you want to have, which will help you take more productive actions and save time.

Regularly reviewing the Goal Highlighter helps you spot goals that change. This is normal. For example, sometimes people set a goal to change a job, only to realize that they can achieve an internal promotion which they find preferable. Many times goals can also start off as rather vague notions that only crystallize with time. So do not worry if you have trouble expressing some of your goals. Start with what you can name and review regularly. If your goal becomes clearer, note the new goal and adjust your actions to reach it.

14

BE PRODUCTIVE ACROSS ALL YOUR KEY PRIORITIES

Overall happiness and satisfaction come from a sense of balanced productivity in the various domains of our lives that are important. The Total Productivity Wheel is a very popular exercise within the coaching community. It encourages you to examine your satisfaction with a number of life areas so that action can be taken to rectify specific areas of imbalance or dissatisfaction.

The wheel will help you develop awareness about where you are now and what action you want to take, and will help you track your progress. The exercise highlights clearly where things are, what's important, what the key priorities are and what specifically will be done to improve things. It provides a tangible framework for an unconscious process that goes on in your mind in the background and which, for some people, can be very tiring. By working with the information in front of you, examining what you have and want, your mind will automatically create ideas about actions you can take to improve results. Having things written down can also free your mind from having to continuously think about everything and instead allows your brain to focus on coming up with specific strategies and steps you can use to take action.

Completing this exercise will help you boost your productivity, identify specific blockers to action, help you acknowledge and celebrate your achievements and, most importantly, help you create action plans to support forward movement. For maximum results, I recommend that a new wheel is done every one to two months depending on the number of action points.

TOTAL PRODUCTIVITY WHEEL EXERCISE

1. Look around the wheel and the categories and decide those you want to keep. Replace and/or add any further areas that need to be represented, or subtract from it in a way that fits your current circumstances. You may wish to construct separate wheels that are purely work- or life-based. Once you have your broad wheel, consider whether you wish to further subdivide specific sections to help you. For example, you may wish to subdivide physical environment into home and work, as both are important environments where you spend a good deal of time. Friends and family might also deserve to be subdivided. It doesn't matter how many slices you have as long as they are the key bits in your life that matter. Sometimes you begin with one category and on subsequent visits you might decide that it needs further subdividing.

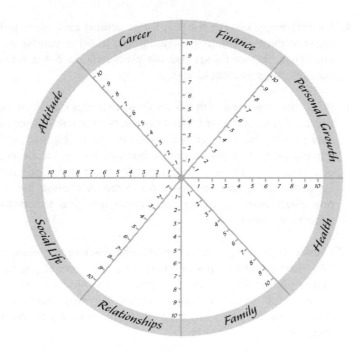

2. Once you are happy with your overall wheel, go around and give each area a score out of 10 that corresponds to your satisfaction with how productive you are in each area. The scores will change over time, so it helps to label each wheel exercise with a date to remind you when you completed it.

3. As you give each category a score, pay attention to what is making you give it that score. In your mind you will have a picture or idea of some standard that equates with a score of 10 and you will be evaluating your current state against it. Absolute numerical accuracy is not so important. For example, it matters little if it's a 2 or 3, a 6 or 7. Go with your gut.

4. For reference, keep a running list of actions and ideas that come to mind of things that could help to bring your scores up. These are not things you will absolutely do but a list of possible steps you could take.

5. When you are done with the whole wheel, take a look at the overall shape. Is it even? What are the high scores? What do they provide for you? How did they get to be high scores? Sometimes certain areas are low but they turn out to be less of a priority than others. That is fine. We need a manageable list of items that we can focus on to create change and at any given time we always pay more attention to certain aspects of our life.

6. Identify three categories within the wheel where you want to take action and list specific things you can commit yourself to doing/changing within these areas to increase your score. Some of the ideas will come from the list you generated in step 4. This creates a simple to-do list for the time period in question.

Notes:

7. Pick a time frame for your action points: four weeks, two months, etc. and then check that your actions can be achieved in that window of time. Be ambitious but also realistic.

Reflective Questions

- When you look across your own productivity wheel what does it tell you about what you find easy or easier and what you find more challenging?
- Which part of the wheel is most neglected and what implication does this have for your overall happiness, your confidence and your wellbeing?
- Suppose your productivity wheel was evenly balanced and had top scores all around. What would this look and feel like on a daily basis? What is more useful for you to aim for, perfection in some areas or working towards developing a more even balance across all your key areas?

 BE PRODUCTIVE ACROSS ALL YOUR KEY PRIORITIES: TAKEAWAY LESSONS

After doing this exercise you should be able to assess your overall productivity and keep it in balance as you focus and take actions in all areas that are important to you. Repeated on a regular basis, the wheel will help you keep momentum and motivate you to stay productive. This is especially true when you note down your next action steps. These will, for the most part, suggest themselves as you work through each area. Trust your mind.

Action steps should stretch you and energize you. Piling on so much that most of it gets left undone will undermine your confidence and sense of achievement. You should equally watch out for action steps that are simply too big. Writing down big steps that will involve many substeps tends to demotivate and create an unrealistic plan because it will be too difficult to tick off the big items for some time. This can easily seduce your mind into negative thoughts and make progress seem impossible, which will sabotage your success. What's needed is a series of action steps in each area that can be completed relatively easily or immediately.

Taking small but specific actions builds momentum and advances progress. The mind will automatically identify the next step for each area and the one after that. It is not important to know all the steps, only enough to get going. Many people feel good recording small steps as part of their progress. From much experience I think this is a good habit, as it provides another layer of clear evidence for your eyes and mind that the effort expended is yielding clear results. This is especially key on large projects. Choose whatever method works best for you. It should be one that can clearly tell you what you need to do next, reaffirm for you that your work is taking you forward and allow you to determine if your goals are likely to be met or if you need to tweak what you're doing.

Done correctly, the Total Productivity Wheel will help reveal areas where actions perhaps don't happen as quickly as you think they should, where they are more difficult for you or where the relative level of importance of this area compared with others is low. By studying your productivity wheel, you will be able to determine your own success strategies for creating progress and balance them to achieve holistic productivity. You might find and confirm that you simply took too much on and it's a question of learning how to manage your time better. Or it may reveal lack of a specific skill or attitude to take certain actions. Of course, the counterpart is also true. Systematic completion of a wheel on a regular basis will highlight your specific strengths and goals that really spur you on. When you have completed a few Total Productivity Wheel exercises over some time, you will also be able to see just how much you have moved forward and how much you have learned and developed. That is a gift that keeps on giving. By working around the whole wheel systematically you will be taking some action in all areas, thus keeping yourself balanced and healthy.

15

WORK OUT WHERE YOUR ACTIONS ARE TAKING YOU

One of the key bits of awareness required to create amazing results is an explicit understanding of your regular patterns of activities. Knowing how you spend your time in practice is invaluable in being able to make conscious decisions about your future and often about what you choose to do in the present. When you look at how you spend time now in comparison to how you would like your day to look ideally, you can begin to make specific changes that will create the results you desire. In fact, often the mind is doing that automatically, except that when the process is taking place in our subconscious state, the result takes longer and it can be difficult to believe that change is possible.

Time Travel is a useful exercise to help generate this information in a clear way, as it highlights what you are moving towards unconsciously or whether you are stuck. When you see what is happening, your brain can begin to make decisions about what to do. The exercise is based on the belief that you are always aiming to create a state which meets your needs, values and goals and which makes you happy. Any patterns, positive or negative, that are revealed in this exercise are worth exploring. Patterns or trends provide rich information for making positive adjustments sooner.

1. Consider what your day looks like over a 24-hour period using the circles below. Sketch your typical work and leisure day. Half of the circle is twelve hours, a quarter is six hours, and so on.

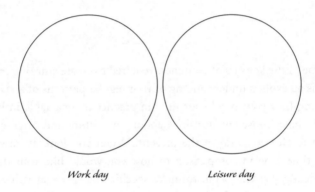

Work day   Leisure day

2. To generate a picture of where time goes at the moment, begin by filling in/shading the typical values of time you devote to the following activities:
sleep
work
personal hygiene
meals
travel/commute
shopping
chores/tasks
wellbeing activities such as sports, hobbies
learning
time with others.

If there are other things you do, please account for them in your circles. Once you have a wheel showing where your time goes, you will be able to see how much free time is left (if any).

3. How satisfied are you with your circles in terms of how you spend your time, from 0 (completely dissatisfied) to 10 (very satisfied)? Note down any small changes you may wish to make.

Notes:

4. You are now ready for time travel as you look back and forward at the same picture.

5. **Looking back**
   What did each day look like two, three, five years ago? Pick a time that makes most sense for you. You may pick more than one and repeat the exercise for both time periods from the past.

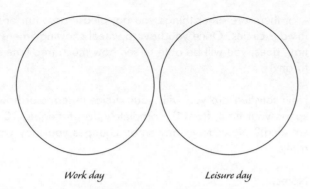

Work day   *Leisure day*

What has changed and what remains the same in the way you spend your work and leisure time between the past and now? What does this reveal for you in terms of your habits, needs or patterns, good and bad?

6. Looking forward
How will the picture look a year, two, three, five years from now in your opinion? Again, pick a time frame that fits your circumstances.

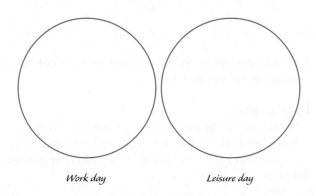

Work day   *Leisure day*

Go back through each pair of circles and see how closely they correspond to your ideal way of spending your work and leisure time. If you had to go around your circles and assign smiley faces to these activities and their time allocation, would you find any frowns and why? What do you want to do to change this?

Notes:

Reflective Questions

- What is similar and different between work and leisure days? Are you getting enough rest?
- Is there anything that tends to fragment or otherwise negatively impact on your work or leisure days? If so, what do you want to do about it?
- What actions can you take to improve how you spend time now in order to achieve what you want in your future?
- Have you got something that either adds joy and happiness to your life or helps you sustain your energy in your work and leisure day? If not, what could that be?

WORK OUT WHERE YOUR ACTIONS ARE TAKING YOU: TAKEAWAY LESSONS

Being able to see clearly what is happening to you over time by becoming a conscious observer provides a powerful new window of awareness. Hopefully the Time Travel exercise has helped you identify specific preferences for activities and time allocations (desirable and less desirable), patterns of behaviour you adopt over time and in some cases the optimal lifestyle that you are trying to create. The information you have gained will provide you with a good picture of the life you are creating. Is it the life you want? If not, change it!

Hopefully your trajectory and trend is a positive one, i.e. your work and leisure times are staying constantly good or are improving. Many people find that they are always moving towards what they truly want. The speed and the boldness of the moves, however, can often be severely hampered by unhelpful beliefs, deep fears, lack of safety and past failures. Life is designed to be actually pretty amazing. It takes courage and conscious decisions to make it so. Do you like how you spend your time? If not, change it! If yes, well done you!

SECTION THREE

NOT GOOD ENOUGH!

I can recall all too well the many times when I heard the voice of doubt in my head stopping me from pursuing specific goals or sabotaging my efforts. Over the last few years though, that same voice has become my friend. Working on many professional turnarounds and helping people realize their potential, I have learned how to use 'not good enough' as a motivator to raise standards and performance. As a result, I expect more from myself and from others but I do so with kindness, appreciation and love. Like top-level consultants, together we use facts to learn and improve continuously. In doing so, we proactively allow others to help us do better and live a more productive life. Our brains are marvellous at affecting our thoughts and our behaviour. In my observations, brains are wired for productivity. All we need is to learn to work with what they tell us. If you carry a voice of doubt or wish to raise your confidence, the exercises in this section will help you discover how to control and, in fact, leverage the strength of your powerful mind to help you to be productive. It all begins in your mind.

16

FACE YOUR PRODUCTIVITY ALLY

Somewhere in our brain sits a little productivity ally. He or she periodically sends us messages about how we are doing. At times these are positive, motivational vibes in the form of 'Wow, I'm really doing it!' or 'Can't believe I got it all done!'. At other times, though, the messages are critical and limiting. The voice might say things like: 'You'll never get this done' or 'It won't work' or 'You're stupid and slow', 'You can't handle it.'

Think for a moment how these words make you feel. Both sets of statements are useful but many people pay far more attention to the negative ones than the positives. This, in part, explains why many people have difficulty in getting started but less so in continuing a given activity. It is much harder to ignore a voice that says 'You can't' before you even begin. Once you begin, though, the voice often joins in a positive assertion of 'I'm doing it' or simply goes away.

The Productivity Ally exercise gives you a chance to identify what your productivity ally is looking for, where and what he or she frequently says to you and to consider how he or she is influencing your productivity. The objective of getting to know your productivity ally is that you can get him or her to help you. At times, it may feel like the put downs are intentionally there to stop you, make you feel guilty and/or criticize you. However, the productivity ally does this because fundamentally it thinks you can do better. It's effectively a harsh but effective coach. It wants you to succeed. It just needs to be schooled!

The information that you will generate in this exercise will give you a powerful insight into the yardsticks and benchmarks the controller uses, which might need to be renegotiated, as well as helping you develop better communication skills that you can apply to create productive relationships with yourself and with others.

PRODUCTIVITY ALLY EXERCISE

1. **Get to know your productivity ally**

   When does your inner productivity ally show up and what does he or she say to you? For example, what would the voice point out to you, what would it say about how productive you are, what you're doing well and what you're doing badly or avoiding? Make a list of all the statements that come to mind.

   Notes:

2. Write a description of your productivity ally
What does he or she look like if you can imagine it? What does he or she wear? Does he or she share characteristics or resemble someone you know? You may wish to draw them or depict them with a caricature or a character.

It may help for you to get into their skin for a while and observe them from inside. How do they view the world and is it different from you?

Notes:

3. Embrace your productivity ally
Think about what his or her positive intention is instead of what it says to you. What is he or she trying to help ensure you do or achieve?

Use this information to help you take better action.

Notes:

4. Build a master productivity allies team
If you can think of external people in your life whose advice, comments or perspective often show up for you, use them as

extra productivity allies and consider how what they say can help you instead of block you. Could what they say be used to help you check your facts, develop extra caution or take a risk, for example?

5. **Become more productive with the help of the key productivity gurus in your life**
   Which people in your life (those you know directly and those you may only know from a distance) exhibit characteristics, achievements or habits that appear highly productive? This could be in how they get things done, network, communicate, etc. What do they appear to be doing? Which of these would be helpful in your life to model/adopt?

6. **Collect and consider your various allies**
   Now that you know who your allies are, note down specific changes you think might be useful to make.

   Notes:

 Reflective Questions

- What information or evidence does your inner productivity ally pay attention to most? What's important for him or her? You may wish to think about the comparisons or benchmarks he or she uses to evaluate or judge you. Are they grounded in facts and reasonable? What does your ally fail to take into account?

- When did your productivity ally first appear? How did you ever manage without him or her? What does this tell you?
- In what situations or areas of your life are any of these productivity allies most useful? When would checking in with them be most beneficial?
- In what situations, if any, do you adopt the voice of your productivity ally with others? What effect does this have on them and on your relationship? If the impact is negative, can you find alternative ways of being supportive to others?

 ### FACE YOUR PRODUCTIVITY ALLY: TAKEAWAY LESSONS

It might seem hard at first but your productivity ally is a part of you and it deserves your respect because it is there to help you be your best. We can't embrace something unless we can recognize its value and believe it is there to help us instead of being out to get us. Your ally is there to help you.

Our brains are extremely powerful. They can't help but judge and compare, and our tacit knowledge is wide. We know far more than we think we know. By working with this material, you will help turn this energy and resource into productivity and high-level results without becoming a totally debilitating perfectionist or a perpetual life critic. You will learn to use those skills for the good they are intended for: which is to help you do your best! Occasionally, people doing this exercise discover that they have more than one productivity ally. If this happened to you, don't panic. Repeat the exercise for each separate controller voice you still carry within you, so that you end up building a team of internal helpers. Set them tasks and challenges to bring you answers that support you moving forward.

Given the positive intention of your productivity ally, hopefully you have figured out useful ways in which he or she and you can work together to help you move forward constructively. Instead of using the voice to stop you, you can use what it tells you as a valuable perspective to check in with yourself and improve your performance. You may need to listen hard for what he or she says. Negotiate with him or her. Allow a bit of internal dialogue to take place. You're not going crazy! You are simply realigning parts of you so that they work with your mind rather than against it. Don't be scared of your productivity ally. It is but a tiny fraction of who you are. If you uncovered one in yourself, you hopefully discovered that it joined you at some stage in your life as a result of specific experiences. It wasn't there at the start and you can get on in the world perfectly without it. So its presence is there to help you for a while, to learn and become stronger and to do your best.

Finally, you might have found that you indeed sound like a productivity ally to others in real life or specific situations – perhaps as a partner, boss or a colleague. Having considered the effects of this style of managing performance with yourself, I hope the exercise has helped you consider options for changing what you say and how. When others receive what you see as help, they should see it as help too.

I have no doubt that this exercise will provide you with a wealth of information and insight to help you achieve top-level results without the hassle and heartache of internal controllers that, when ignored, can get out of hand. This will set you far apart and help you succeed.

17

USE YOUR EMOTIONS TO
GENERATE POSITIVE RESULTS

Emotions play a big role in personal productivity. They can accelerate action or bring it to a standstill. Certain emotions can make it difficult to stay motivated and focus on what you want or need to get done. Think about the last time you felt blocked from taking action by how you felt – when you were simply frozen. We've all been there. It is at those points in time that we learn the most and grow as people, although, in that moment, it can often feel uncomfortable and frustrating. People who effectively manage their emotions are able to acknowledge them, be with them, learn from them and use them for productivity instead of feeling paralyzed.

Emotions carry with them certain energy states. Some add energy while others take it away. At any given moment, we experience a number of emotions. For example, you can feel happy, expectant, anxious and scared all at the same time. The emotion that often predominates and the one you experience as a mood in that moment is the strongest emotion. If you feel happy, successful, accomplished and healthy but in the moment are feeling very angry with someone, you may experience anger, for example. Many of the other emotions that you feel concurrently go unnoticed. So, while the other emotions are present and run in the background, without tuning into them consciously, i.e. looking for them, the emotion that you're mostly conscious of at the moment is anger. This might leave you with the risk of unconsciously giving up control and letting anger control and dictate what you do and how you act. I can assure you, you won't like the results and it won't really be you! Because anger is not all you feel.

The Emotional Palette is a quick and effective self-awareness exercise to generate insight about all the emotions that present themselves in the moment and to use this knowledge to paint a more accurate picture of how you are feeling. This is especially key when experiencing emotions that strongly and negatively affect your actions. By tuning into what you're feeling, all your emotions, however weak, can be mapped out in front of you so that you can notice them, own them and consciously choose the emotion that best serves you in that moment. This means that you won't be hijacked by powerful emotions. Instead, you will use them to help you take effective action and develop as a productive person. If you find yourself having trouble describing your feelings or getting in touch with them, this exercise will help you to develop your emotional side.

EMOTIONAL PALETTE EXERCISE

1. Think of your emotions at any given moment as an artistic palette. You are painting your reality with the emotions that are present at any given moment in time. Tune into what you are feeling right this minute, and listen in for all the emotions that exist within you. When you become aware of one, name it and write it down. Some emotions will be strong and obvious. Be patient. Allow the weaker emotions to have a voice too. Your job is to capture all of the emotions present

within you at this point in time. They are all equally valid emotions.

Notes:

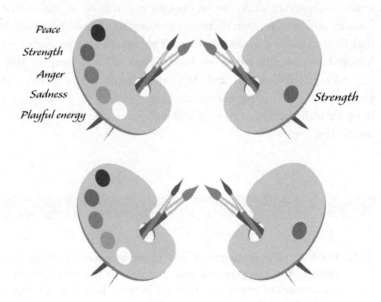

2. Examine each emotion in turn and the mental state and resourcefulness level it provides you with at this moment. What does this emotion do for you? What is it here to teach you/remind you of? What does it tell you about yourself?

Own each one as they are all a part of you. As you do this you may notice the powerful emotions weaken in intensity as you restore balance to your emotional palette.

Notes:

3. Now, consciously pick an emotion from your palette that would be most useful for you to adopt in whatever you would like to do next. Which emotion would best serve you? It doesn't mean you are leaving the others behind. You still own them all. You are, however, making a conscious choice about how the emotions will affect you. When you make a choice, commit to it and own it.

Notes:

 Reflective Questions

- What are you learning about emotions in general? What do you think is their purpose?
- What is your attitude to your various emotions after this exercise? If you feared some of them before, has that fear lessened perhaps?

- If you look back in time, what emotions have tended to predominate for you? How is this serving you? Is this a conscious choice or an accident?
- Consider people you're interacting with on a regular basis. If you had to take a guess, what would their emotional palette look like? How can you positively influence their palette?
- How can you use this knowledge for building more effective relationships with others and yourself?

 ## USE YOUR EMOTIONS TO GENERATE POSITIVE RESULTS: TAKEAWAY LESSONS

What you feel is your reality. It is your truth. If you choose to ignore it, you will cause yourself suffering. This is why having a healthy relationship with your emotional palette (all the things you are feeling) is very important for your long-term success and for being authentic.

Once mastered, this exercise can be completed in seconds and will help you manage all sorts of situations. You will be able to manage the contradictory emotional states that can leave other people confused or even paralyzed and use them as the guidance and signals they are meant to offer you. I have seen this exercise mastered by my clients, and its power cannot be overstated. With time, it will help you become more grounded in yourself and have the confidence to own and deal with your emotions as well as becoming more sensitive to the emotions of others.

18

UNLOCK YOUR PERSPECTIVE TO MAKE BETTER DECISIONS

At any given point, we view the world from a specific perspective or point of view. So, this is a position or mindset you adopt in any given situation. Of course, each situation or circumstance can be viewed from many different perspectives. For example, what would the world look like if you chose to see it as a game, or a party or a glass ceiling that can be smashed away with ease? Whether it is a characteristic of a person or a situation, we choose the way we look at it and the meaning we create or extract from it. Each perspective will determine what it is that we see, think and feel. Each is a version of reality but not reality itself.

To make better choices and decisions and create more productive states, it is often useful to become aware of the perspective that your mind adopts or one in which it might be *stuck*. Until we consciously acknowledge how we are viewing something, we risk being blinded by the tunnel vision of a limited and single perspective. This means you could be blocking sufficient choices and options, and your ability to make a good decision will be severely impaired. Also, by not truly examining all the choices available, you could end up forcing a choice prematurely. Often the feeling of 'being stuck' comes about when an individual or a group gets locked into viewing something from a perspective that is simply not very helpful. They might make a decision that doesn't sit well with them or which they can't really own. By bringing awareness to the perspective you are in, and also by adopting other perspectives, you can systematically generate additional options and greatly improve how you handle most situations.

The Alternative Perspective exercise is a useful technique for generating additional options and possibilities and identifying more resourceful states for action that resonate with you. The technique is relatively simple and, once mastered, can be performed in minutes.

ALTERNATIVE PERSPECTIVE EXERCISE

1. Pick an issue, challenge or situation you are facing where you could benefit from having further options. Write it down on a piece of paper so that it is in the middle.

2. Consider how you are viewing the issue right now. If you had to give it a name, what perspective are you in? For example, you might be in your critical mode or a joking mode, etc. Write this down as the first perspective. Note down what seems possible from here. Tune into what you hear when in this perspective. What emotions come up?

3. Now imagine another perspective, perhaps that of a best friend or someone who deeply cares about you. Step into this position and look at the issue from here. What is possible, different or new in this space? Note down your thoughts and ideas.

Notes:

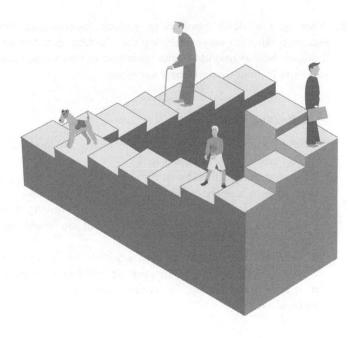

4. Continue to make up additional perspectives and repeat steps 1–3 for each one. View the situation from each perspective and note down what's possible there. Don't be afraid to get creative with your perspectives. You may wish to pick random objects, characters or places and challenge yourself to find associations and links you never thought existed. When you occupy each perspective you begin to see the world or a specific situation from more angles. If two perspectives become similar, merge them into one so that each perspective offers you a distinct space and a different set of options or ideas.

5. When you're done generating various perspectives and exploring different ways of seeing the situation, pick the one that feels best in relation to the issue and decide what action you want to take that will best serve you.

 Reflective Questions

- What happened to the number of options you generated as you added new perspectives?
- Is the best perspective the one you started with or have you been able to identify a more resourceful perspective?
- How do you feel about the choice you made having gone through this exercise in comparison to what you would have done without it?
- In what other situations in your work/life at the moment would unlocking your perspective be helpful? It could be a specific relationship, a career decision, a business venture, etc.

 ## UNLOCK YOUR PERSPECTIVE TO MAKE BETTER DECISIONS: TAKEAWAY LESSONS

When you examine a situation or a problem from a number of per-spectives you unlock your thinking. You notice things you were not paying attention to before. Sometimes these are useful and at times they can be critical. You may also notice that what you thought or wanted to do was hugely affected by how you perceived the situation at the start, perhaps too much so. Once you return a balance to what is, you often discover that you may need more information, or that some of the assumptions you made are just that – assumptions instead of reality.

Often a useful perspective turns out to be something remote, bizarre or seemingly unrelated, such as a favourite dessert, a perfume, an imaginary object or a certain character (either real or imaginary). The mind is wonderful at creating all the links it needs to draw the necessary parallels. So don't shy away from experimenting with seemingly wacky ideas for perspectives. How would your neighbours' golden lab Charlie see the situation?

This considered way of thinking can really transform what you achieve and how you approach and handle different situations, as it generates more ideas. Sometimes, you may go through this exercise and discover that what you thought initially still applies. If that is true, then considering the situation from a number of perspectives gives you the advantage of further certainty. With time you will develop a habit of routinely considering various perspectives, which will help you to become more resourceful in your actions and decision making. As you begin to open your eyes to other ways of seeing things, you will also build more productive relationships with other people.

19

UNDERSTAND HOW YOUR BRAIN HELPS YOU TO BE PRODUCTIVE

Emotions are the brain's signals or messages for action or information that you can use to help you make better decisions. They are a product of your brain thinking about stuff on a conscious and subconscious level. Your brain constantly absorbs loads and loads of information from everything that surrounds you. It learns and stores information, which it can call on to help you make sense of new experiences and to help you learn. The mind constantly relates the world out there to what it knows.

Some signals are like traffic lights. They are easy to interpret. They give the brain a clear 'Go', 'Caution' or 'Stop' signal. Others can be more confusing. All emotions have a role to play and carry useful information. Much time can be saved and confusion avoided by knowing the code your emotions use.

For example, the emotion of Fear is a very useful signal to alert us that we need to prepare. Once we know that, we can look at what we fear and focus on creating appropriate plans for managing that situation. This makes fear diminish in size or can make it disappear. Many people with phobias are afraid of things without actually needing to experience them because they can visualize what they fear. Thus, fear prevents them from having the actual experience and being able to manage or conquer their fear. Fear is largely about control. When a person has control over the situation, their fear lessens. So the signal to fear is actually a highly valuable brain code that tells us to take action and create plans to give us more control of a highly uncertain and potentially dangerous situation or one that is simply unpredictable. What about feeling bored? When we're not sufficiently stimulated, our brain is sending us a signal. It tells us that it's wasting time where it could be having fun or working on something worthwhile.

Generally the negative emotions will cause you to stop and the positive ones to keep going. But the emotional world is far more complicated than that. Imagine what would happen if you always stopped at things that made you nervous or caused you anxiety. Your world would be getting smaller instead of larger and that is not how productive people work.

The Emotional Code is an action short cut exercise that will help you understand how your brain talks to you. Once you know this, you will be able to use your emotional states productively. You will be able to extract the meaning behind the emotion and take appropriate action without having to sacrifice your goals and dreams for the wrong reasons.

EMOTIONAL CODE EXERCISE

1. Note down an emotion that gets in the way of what you want to achieve or which clouds your ability to get things done well. Some examples of these include: frustration, anger, disappointment and procrastination.

   Notes:

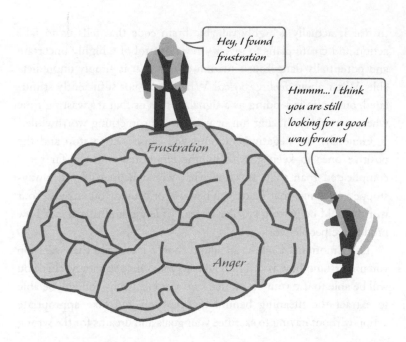

2. Think about a specific situation when you felt this emotion and then zero in on the moment when you finally took *action*.

3. Note down the action you eventually took that was productive or helped move you forward. It doesn't matter how long it took you to act as long as the action you took felt really right for you in your heart and in your head. This is key!

Notes:

4. Examine other times when you felt the same emotion and note down the action you eventually took. Note whether the same sort of action appears consistently with this emotion. For example, the action may involve seeking information, switching your focus, talking to someone, etc.

Notes:

5. Now connect the emotion with the actions to derive your own emotional code for this emotion. So, if you felt a high level of uncertainty and spent a long time delaying, ruminating over something until you eventually went and gathered more information, then your uncertainty code simply says: gather more information right away instead of waiting.

6. Repeat the steps above for other emotions. You may also go through the exercise to decode the effect your 'positive' emotions have on your behaviour for clues about how to use them when you want to or need them to get things done.

 Reflective Questions

- What are you learning about your emotional codes? How predictable is the code for you?
- Which emotions keep you trapped for long periods of time in an unproductive activity? What will you be able to do now?

- Are there specific situations in your life right now where you can use the decoded emotional message your brain is sending you to help you take a concrete step forward?
- If you look around you – your place of work, your partner or key client – can you spot emotions that are trapping you in an unproductive state? If so, knowing what you know now, what's the code?

 ## UNDERSTAND HOW YOUR BRAIN HELPS YOU TO BE PRODUCTIVE: TAKEAWAY LESSONS

I hope you can now begin to appreciate how useful emotions really are and that the exercise inspires you to stay in touch with what you feel on a regular basis. This will save you valuable time and help you make sense of the world around you. If you choose to ignore your emotions, you are truly depriving yourself of lots of richness. Your brain is there to help you. Talk about your emotions. This will let other people develop a greater understanding and appreciation of your uniqueness. You have nothing to be embarrassed about. People who are in touch with their emotional side have greater depth and experience life more fully. Using your emotional code means you don't dwell in emotional land, you use it to thrive.

20
TAKE CONTROL OF YOUR FEAR

Fear is a very powerful emotion. It can keep us in a prison and away from the things we want with all our heart either professionally or in our personal life. Fear is a real conundrum. Sometimes, we want something very much and yet we fear it equally strongly and we jeopardize it or walk away from an opportunity because we allow fear to take over. Overcoming fear, or at least controlling its impact on your life and success, is important and it is largely about developing awareness about what you truly fear and then developing a safety net through planning. Take people at work who fear they will lose their job. Fear of job loss can be debilitating but ultimately unproductive. What is productive is getting your CV updated and taking actions to prepare alternative posts or ideally a better role to walk away to on your terms.

Fear is just another of the brain's codes. Its function is a warning system about potential danger. When you face something that presents risk, fear is the signal for your brain to consider the situation more carefully, aim to understand it and then take well-reasoned and appropriate action. Too often, however, fear causes an immediate reaction that, in many cases, is inappropriate and at times damaging to our happiness and interpersonal relationships.

Where there is fear between people, interactions are unhealthy, whether in business or personal relationships. Fear destroys collaboration, friendship and business. When we experience fear we do not trust. Instead we expend energy in second-guessing people's motives, worrying about losing out, playing head games and generally engaging in unproductive behaviours to protect ourselves from what we fear. Instead of facing and addressing the fear to make ourselves more effective, we waste valuable time and risk hurting others and ourselves in the process, and often jeopardize good outcomes. When we let fear overtake us, we stop communicating with the other person or seeing the situation as it is. Instead we communicate with the junk fear installs in our brains and work with our imagination instead of reality.

There is one magic thing that makes fear lessen or disappear, and that is safety. When you feel safe, you trust and a lot of the junk in your mind goes away, allowing you to stay in the moment, think productively and make good decisions. When you feel safe in relationships you know that you can be honest with the other person and trust that you can work through challenges together as a team. When there's team safety, people focus on the task instead of personal agendas and when there's trust in a company, staff get on with the job, excel and thrive.

The Fear Safety Net exercise is designed to help you identify your fears so that you remain or become more productive. Once you understand what you fear exactly, you can begin to create appropriate safety nets to support your success and help you to get what you want without letting fear keep you away from it. No matter how small a start you make, in time you will not believe how much more you will accomplish – that's what being productive is all about.

FEAR SAFETY NET EXERCISE

1. Think about your life right now and what generally makes you experience fear. You may have a long list or you might find it hard to come up with something to start with. Be patient. Think about things you might fear doing but would like to. This may include things you want to say or do, things

you wanted to do before but stopped short of or things that you perhaps are not prepared for and which would cause you a great deal of fear were they to happen. For each item that you wish to consider further and begin to address, continue with the questions below.

Notes:

2. Having described your fear in detail, note down what exactly is at risk in this situation. What do you stand to lose? What are you hoping to protect? List everything you can think of, big or small.

Notes:

3. If you think about a specific situation where this fear shows up, does it help you take actions and behave in a way that moves you closer to what you really want or does it take you away from what you would like ideally to happen?

Notes:

4. Note down what you could do or what would be possible if your fear didn't exist or simply went away.

Notes:

5. Note down what safety net you would need to have in place to make the fear lessen or go away entirely within this situation. What would you need to see, hear, feel or have? This may include specific things you must have or people that might be able to help you. What would you need to assume or believe to help you manage your fear? Is there a leap of faith you could take, and what would make that possible? Alternatively, note down what would make the situation safe. For example, I can speak in public if I practise with my colleagues and they are in the audience to support me.

Notes:

6. Write down what you need to do to create your safety net, however small. As your safety net strengthens, your fear will lessen, so be patient. Note specific actions and implement them.

Notes:

Reflective Questions

- Is there someone else you need to talk to about your fear? For example, if this fear involves another person or people, being able to say what you fear will enable others to help you. Remember, everyone fears. It's a completely normal emotion.
- Can you think about other places where fear is getting in the way of what is desired? How could this fear be managed?
- What safety net do you create when you have to communicate a difficult message to others? This could involve people close to you as well as your clients, colleagues and even people you hardly know. What would a safety net look like there?
- How can you measure/keep track of your progress in handling what you fear so that you see your growth and progress? What are some specific benefits to you when you can face your fears? Are there any benefits for others around you that you can anticipate also? If so, what are they?

TAKE CONTROL OF YOUR FEAR: TAKEAWAY LESSONS

Productive people don't let fear stop them. Instead they learn to manage it and work to overcome it. With each step forward, their confidence grows and their fear lessens. Every person fears something. You are not alone. The fear might be conceptual or based on previous experiences. However it arose doesn't matter and I would suggest you don't explore its origin in this exercise. What is key is that you name what it is in detail and begin to see it and handle it for what it is. Not something large and overwhelming but something that, however big, can be broken down into specific descriptors that you can tackle by planning safety measures.

111

Safety nets need not be permanent. In fact, in many situations, they only need to be ensured in the interim so that you can gain the trust you need to move forward. As you take each step you might become aware of new safety nets that you need, and so on. This is normal. Remember, trust happens in degrees and all journeys result from taking one step at a time. Every now and then you might be prepared to leap forward, but if this is not your style, then creating gradual safety platforms for yourself might suit you best and help ensure your fear is not sabotaging your success.

By doing this exercise you have taken an important step in building up your resilience and risk-taking skills. Planning your safety nets and creating those support mechanisms, whether in conversations or situations, is vital for success. They help you relax and feel confident instead of out of control. If your fear is connected to other people, talking about fear itself will definitely help build trust. As you reach out to others and choose to show your vulnerability to them, you will be building trust with them and inviting them to trust you too. This will deepen your relationships and allow you to tackle difficult conversations.

Managing fear is a courageous act and an ongoing practice. Start slowly and trust that, with each step, you are getting stronger! Keep going. Return to this exercise periodically to note your progress and identify new challenges. I guarantee that, with time, you will find you are much stronger and more courageous than when you started.

21

FOLLOW YOUR WANTs INSTEAD OF YOUR MUSTs

If you think about the things you have achieved or created in your life up to now that you chased and chased and which consumed loads of your effort and yet left you happy, it is most likely that you really wanted those things to happen. It could be that ambitious job you really wanted, your own business or someone you asked out on a date. Human beings can't help but want certain things, and the more they want them, the more they are prepared to do to obtain them. This means that WANTs carry a lot of power within them to help motivate action and resourcefulness.

All of us also have certain MUSTs in our lives. For example, we know that we MUST eat well if we want to perform at our best. We MUST breathe to live.

Whereas WANTs are internally driven, i.e. they come from within us, MUSTs tend to come from the outside world. One way or another they are imposed on us. They may take the form of expectations, norms or rules. MUSTs often get expressed as 'oughts' and 'shoulds' as well. WANTs only have one word for them.

What is key when you want to realize powerful results is to follow your WANTs instead of your MUSTs. True WANTs are so powerful that they become a way of being.

The WANTs exercise is an honest check-in exercise to help you capture what's true for you right now and discover what you want instead of what you should want. This means that you can develop awareness about what makes the 'should wants' different and why, at times, you do them instead of what you really want to do. The exercise will help you uncover how your mind thinks and makes decisions and hopefully give you the right insights about what you need to change if you're spending all your time in the land of MUSTs instead of WANTs.

WANTS EXERCISE

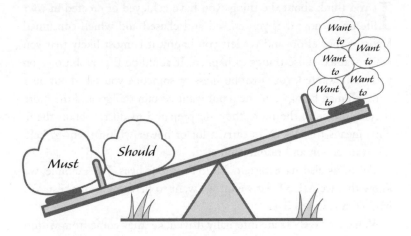

1. Make a list of your current MUSTs on one side of a page and a list of your real WANTs on the other side.

2. How do you feel about the MUSTs? Do they evoke feelings of excitement, drive and happiness or do they leave you with a sense of burden? Which MUSTs are serving you well and which are causing you pain/suffering? Are there any MUSTs that are not even critical or vital in the short term? If so, cross them out and drop them.

3. Now look at your WANTs. Note down how each one makes you feel. Are the emotions that come up for you generally more positive than when you considered your MUST activities?

Notes:

4. Note the difference between WANTs you are actively pursuing and those that you're not taking any action on. Note down what's missing for you to move forward on them.

Notes:

 Reflective Questions

- What do your MUSTs and WANTs tell you about what guides what you do at the moment? Is this the way you want things to be? If not, what would it take to change things?
- What is the relationship between your lists of MUSTs and WANTs? Is one a better or worse version of the other? Are there any true alternatives or do your WANTs express completely different aspirations?
- Given how the two columns make you feel, where are you more likely to be truly productive? Where would you prefer to spend most of your time?
- What changes, if any, do you want to make to help you create and lead your life so that you're being and feeling truly productive?

115

FOLLOW YOUR WANTs INSTEAD OF YOUR MUSTs: TAKEAWAY LESSONS

This can be a tough exercise to complete, as it requires you to be very honest with yourself. It will hopefully make you think. Our Western world is overly reliant on materialistic things. We are continuously fed messages loaded with 'shoulds' which we then convert into MUSTs. These can include salary, job titles, status, good looks, certain clothes, etc. They help standardize and pigeonhole individuals into predefined boxes. MUSTs tend to trap people. A MUST that is being done offers something you need. A MUST that is ignored might be good but lacks the necessary attractive energy to inspire action.

I hope this exercise will help remind you that MUSTs are nothing more than external constructs and you have a choice as to whether to buy into them. There are some good MUSTs, such as regular exercise, that can also be difficult to do until they become WANTs.

Sometimes you may have WANTs that you don't act on. This exercise should help you understand what is still missing for you.

One of the best ways to develop a genuine WANT such as losing weight, for example, is to get on with the exercise and pay attention to the positive evidence of getting more fit, looking slimmer, etc. As you see desirable evidence accumulate, positive feelings (so prominent when you want something) develop. I work with many people who want to realize their talents. Those who succeed tap into their passion and drive for the result. Those who remain in a 'MUST' state never get as far. They miss out on all the inspiration and excitement that WANTs offer. Be courageous and follow your true WANTs. Be excited by them and let them spur you on.

22

USE THE POWER OF CRITICISM TO BECOME YOUR TRUE BEST

Western society has become too nice these days. In an effort to be polite, gentle with each other and non-judgemental, there is a tendency to shy away from telling things as they are. We embellish and keep hidden certain truths that are, in fact, the seeds of our future greatness. We forget the power of well-delivered criticism (feedback), which, after all, is there to help! The irony, though, is that we still think it. We just don't say it.

I'm not inviting you to put on a critics' hat and go mad with it. That's a sure fire recipe to lose friends and alienate people. I do, however, hope to inspire you to use criticism as a source of useful information to self-improve and help you succeed.

The Grains of Truth exercise invites you to take a really critical look at yourself and, yes, you guessed it – criticize! It is based on the fact that if you can truly see an area for improvement, then you're probably right. Why else would you think it? The problem is that many people have allowed their inner critic to take over and use this information to harm instead of help. In this exercise, you will discover grains of truth that you can address to help you be your true best. Your confidence will transform from a fragile outer shell into a strong core that will ground you. How else will you become successful other than by being and feeling at your best on the inside?

GRAINS OF TRUTH EXERCISE

1. Take a good, critical look at yourself: what you do, your business, your website, how you show up in key relationships and how you look physically. Now, I'd like you to go ahead and criticize everything you think/feel is wrong with you or what's just not perfect. Note these down in a column, as shown below. This may feel odd or even painful or it may come very easily to you. What's key is that you're doing this to help you grow and be your best.

Grains of truth	How you see yourself	How others see you

2. For each item you noted down, think about what other people (your partner, friends, family, colleagues) would say about you if they were totally honest. Pick the people that fit each item best; if it's work related, pick your colleagues or your boss.

Notes:

3. Now, pause and take a deep breath. You are indeed very brave. You have literally stripped down many masks and pretences and faced your worst truths. I hope you are able

to notice that, actually, it's not as bad as you think. Yes there are things to improve, but life would be boring if you were not a work in progress.

4. At this stage you should have a two-column list and can begin to identify the grains of truth. Take each item in turn and compare the two columns. You might have been harsh in your self-critique or you might have been too soft. It doesn't matter too much. Note down the grains of truth that come through what you said and what you guessed others would say. These will probably take the form of short statements like: 'I need to lose some weight' or 'I'm acting insecure', for example. This is your magic material and starting point from which you will build success.

Notes:

5. Some of the truths will probably be more important than others or more relevant to your success at this point. Circle them. These are the things you need to work on because they are impeding your success. Leave the others behind. They might be true but they are inconsequential at this point.

6. For each truth you decide to address, note down specific action that will help you improve on the situation. Make your actions do-able but significant. Note down the benefits you expect to see/feel when you get there.

Notes:

Reflective Questions

- What did you learn about yourself in this exercise?
- Compare what you see and what others see – what is in agreement and where are the two views different? How can you tell which is more accurate?
- Where do you put more stock – your own view or what you think others see/think about you? Who do you aim to please most?
- What are you telling people at the moment with the way you show up/are? How do you generally appear to them? Is it the real you? Is the picture what you want?

 ## USE THE POWER OF CRITICISM TO BECOME YOUR TRUE BEST: TAKEAWAY LESSONS

Honest feedback and critical self-reflection are crucial for helping you develop into the best version of you. I hope this exercise gave you a lot of insights and ideas for growth towards a more authentic self. Any work you put into this will pay huge dividends in all aspects of your life. You're not meant to address everything in one go. Take it slowly and work diligently on areas that are critical to your success right now.

23

TAKE RESPONSIBILITY FOR WHAT YOU CREATE

When you set a high standard for yourself, whether in a relationship, work, your life or your health, you take responsibility for what *you create*. This is often difficult for people to accept, but the moment you begin to show up in life with this philosophy, things will really change for the better. The extent to which you take responsibility for the results you create becomes your personal responsibility – your PR.

Think about what happens if you see yourself as a 'victim'. All control escapes and a feeling of helplessness and powerlessness ensues. You can create your own circumstances and results – unless you are passive and let them *happen* to you. The choices you make, what you focus your energies on and what you ignore, all help to create specific results. It may not be what you wanted but nonetheless it is a product of the action and decisions you have taken. Each decision opens certain doors and closes others. Results are created. A personal responsibility mindset emphasizes that you look at the role you play in each situation and decide to be proactive. This will help you create the results you want more often.

PERSONAL RESPONSIBILITY (PR) EXERCISE

1. Think of an interaction with a person that is working well. Note down what you think about the person.

Notes:

2. Now, think of a person with whom you don't seem to get on or where the relationship is not as good as it could be. Note down a few key statements that summarize what you honestly think about the person or feel about them.

Notes:

3. Repeat this for a few more people in your life. Pick a mixture of good and less good relationships. How does what you think correlate with whether the relationship works well or not so well?

4. Note down how being in a dysfunctional relationship makes you feel. What emotions tend to surface? Are they positive or do they make the situation worse?

Notes:

5. Revisit a poor relationship and consider what would happen if you adopted some of the things you think and believe about the other person from one of your good relationships.

Notes:

 Reflective Questions

- What do you notice in terms of your responsibility within different relationships?
- What happens to your actions when you're not feeling positive or in control? Are you more prone to reacting to the person or can you remain focused on what you really want in the situation?
- How can you ensure you take more responsibility for the outcomes you create, either in specific situations or within a relationship? Sometimes this means admitting you were wrong or that you're sorry or asking for help. How good are you at doing this?

 TAKE RESPONSIBILITY FOR WHAT YOU CREATE: TAKEAWAY LESSONS

Taking real responsibility within situations is very difficult, especially if you feel frustrated, disappointed or out of control: times when the other person is difficult in your view. Of course, control is an illusion. You have limited control in most situations and interactions. But your brain can fool you into feeling safe when the other person behaves in a way consistent with your expectations. What I hope you notice in this exercise is that to take responsibility for creating effective situations and relationships, you need to be honest about what you really think. If your thinking is not positive, the situation or interaction will be compromised. It becomes harder to aim high and instead you get trapped reconfirming what you think. The situation rarely improves and often gets worse.

When you take responsibility for what happens and apply high standards, you give the situation your very best. You take responsibility and don't let your negative thinking influence your behaviour. Instead you look to find ways in which you can prove yourself wrong. I hope that doing this exercise has helped you notice when you are taking action from a good place within you and when you are getting caught in a spiral of defeatism or negative thinking and compromising your success. As you continue to analyze successful and less positive relationships and situations going forward, I encourage you to notice your own edge of comfort. What do you find super easy and what is difficult? Remember those who learn outperform those who don't. Aim to always take personal responsibility for your bit in a conversation, relationship or situation. Keep learning.

GET PRODUCTIVE AND JUST DO IT!

When I sit down and write a list of things I want to do, or envisage my next big project, I am using my brain to collect information, come up with ideas, create plans, make decisions and take action. Productivity is a choice. A few years ago, I set myself a challenge to help people become more productive by helping them think differently or better in a two-hour workshop that used to take a whole day, and I succeeded. Our brains are made up of billions of nerve cells with massive computational power that has, up to now, been impossible to reproduce in robots. Brains are natural sponges for information they can apply to create solutions. They are designed to learn. Look at kids. They learn so much over a very short amount of time. Learning does not stop when we grow into adults. In fact it becomes easier. A brain is like a muscle. The more you use it, the more fit it becomes. Sadly, as with exercise, thinking requires energy. What I notice working with others is that, often, people feel so busy that they pass up active thinking due to apparent lack of time or by dwelling on 'problems'. This massively compromises their creativity and productivity. The best way to achieve productivity is to actively use your brain. In this section you will pinpoint your productivity blockers, develop lateral thinking and creative storytelling techniques to help you get things done that are important to you. The method I have created has helped a wide range of individuals raise their game, create impressive turnarounds and achieve more than they thought was possible. I'm confident your productivity will soar too.

24

IDENTIFY YOUR
PRODUCTIVITY BLOCKERS

If productivity is about completing the things that you want to do, then the key obstacle to achieving what you want is often linked to time, or so it may appear on the surface. And indeed, there is no shortage of time management books advancing specific systems for filing and prioritizing work as well as teaching you specific habits and tips on how to deal with the ever-increasing list of tasks. They are each valid and good in their own right, as people have different preferences and what works for one person will completely fail with another.

The system I'd like to introduce to you in this section taps into how minds work naturally when we are kids. Children focus on what they want. Adults focus on problems. Kids explore, make mistakes and learn through feedback. Adults generally prefer to copy, fear mistakes and forgo learning. Once you get your head around using your brain as you did when you were a kid, you will be able to overcome any of your individual productivity blockers in a way that meets your requirements and gives you what you want. In fact, you will find that many of the best productivity strategies when deployed in their most effective form are grounded in that way of thinking.

The following are the most common productivity blockers that adults report when they want to improve their time management and achieve more results from their hard-applied effort.

- Procrastinating
- Attempting too much
- Email and paperwork
- Interruptions
- Inadequate planning
- Lack of delegation
- Committed time to other work
- Lack of resolve
- Stress
- Too many meetings
- Poor prioritizing
- No clear goals
- Being too disorganized
- Too much socializing
- Not completing
- Ineffective communication
- Feeling overwhelmed
- Lacking motivation/boredom
- Feeling powerless over the work of others

The first four – procrastination, attempting too much, too much paperwork and email and too many interruptions – are the most frequent productivity barriers I have noticed over the last three years. At one point or another, though, most people will experience a combination of most, if not all, of these.

The key bit to staying productive is to know the specific productivity block affecting you at any point and tackle it by focusing on what you want. Think about how a child focuses on having a toy and won't take no for an answer. As adults, our brains come equipped with more information, existing knowledge and the ability to put things together into new patterns that, in practice, become our unique productivity strategies. They are unique because every person is different. How you may go about creating wealth will probably be very different from how I might go about it, and yet we can both easily achieve what we want if we have a strategy that works for who we are, what we know, how we tend to behave and so on. The best way to achieve productivity is to use your brain to overcome productivity barriers and come up with your own ideas for getting what you want.

COMMON PRODUCTIVITY BARRIERS EXERCISE

1. Select one productivity barrier you are facing at this time from the list above. Create and write down a statement about what it is that you want to achieve. Make it as specific as you can.

Notes:

2. Now give it a time frame. Make it into a realistic task for the time you have, which might be a few hours or a few minutes.

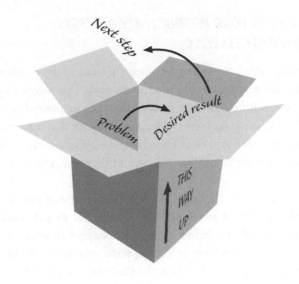

The problem (eeek!)	The desired result (yep!)	The next step (YES!)
I feel totally overwhelmed/ stressed right now.	In the next ten minutes I will write down the top three projects I need to focus on and the specific outcome for each project that tells me what success should look like.	Sit down and write a list.
I'm procrastinating with this report.	Write an outline of the report in the next hour including specific data I will want to use to support my case.	Sit down and write the outline.

IDENTIFY YOUR PRODUCTIVITY BLOCKERS: TAKEAWAY LESSONS

By focusing on what you want to create instead of the problem, your brain will automatically get to productive work. This way you can turn your problem into a desired result. Ensure your desired result is a tangible task that makes sense. The best check for that is to make sure that when you read it back to yourself, it should sound like something you could delegate to another person and they would know what you mean.

This is probably the most powerful differentiator between truly productive people at work and those who fail to get work done. Achievers are able to define specific actions and then get going on them right there and then, or set a specific time to tackle them later. Less productive people dwell on the problem. I hope that, as you do this exercise with your own productivity blockers, you condition your mind to focus on the desired results for a realistic time period that fits your circumstances. It's the oldest trick in the book but many still don't get it. Success is made up of small steps that gradually do add up to those big results. When you define your first step as the big result, though, you will buckle under it and probably derail. So start small and trust that you will get there through steady progress, review and learning as you go.

25

THIRTEEN PROVEN PRODUCTIVITY STRATEGIES YOU NEED TO KNOW

Having the right mindset, as in feeling enthusiastic and generally up to the task, is very useful for being productive. Having high, well-defined standards is good too. However that is not enough. What you also need for high-level productivity is the right strategy to take effective actions that move things forward in a considerable way and create specific desired results.

Imagine wishing to make a tasty recipe and having lots of energy and determination to do it, but not knowing the key ingredients and their amounts. It would be difficult and risky to come up with the right goods on the first try. This is why strategies are so important. A strategy is a protocol of specific steps that creates the desired results every time. What follows is a set of proven productivity strategies that are quite generic until you unleash your brain on them and let them really work!

Let's familiarize ourselves with each one before we begin to play and help you develop your own winning productivity formulas for any context and situation.

STRATEGY 1: COMPLETION

Completion accounts for most of success

What you finish no longer pulls you down

If you are a marathon runner you will really be able to relate to this but you don't need to be one to understand this principle. Most people have far more of a problem with finishing rather than starting work. Often, it is the last 5% that seems to take most time and yet, without it, there is no result. The time invested in starting, though, doesn't count until a piece of work is finished and the result achieved. So completion is really one of the simplest techniques for becoming productive. This strategy will help your brain to identify specifically what needs to be done in order to complete something and then help you turn this into a checklist tool to get it done. Simple and pretty nifty actually! The strategy may also remind you that tasks like marathons require stamina and pacing your energy to allow you to complete the whole run. The same applies to work projects and activities you want to get done.

Completion strategy questions

- How good are you at finishing tasks on a scale from 1 (poor) to 10 (great)?
- What factors affect the score you are at now? What factors would increase it?
- Are there specific contexts where you complete better than others? What gives you the drive in those circumstances?

STRATEGY 2: BULLSEYE PRIORITIZATION

Goal oriented bullseye prioritizing

Plan work so that I finish in x hrs

Sketch a raw project plan with sequence and time estimates

Speak to someone about my plan to check my assumptions and revise if needed

Tackle key incoming requests that need my attention

One important task at a time

One of the key challenges in being productive is focusing on the specific and most important actions and/or results, and making those happen. This becomes a larger challenge as you are called to do more and more, if your job grows without being re-evaluated or if you are pursuing an ambitious and resource-poor project where you may have to wear many hats.

In all of these circumstances, it's easy to end up with long task lists or ideas lists, along with the feeling that no matter how much you do, there is always more to get done in limited time. A great recipe for burn out! These conditions make keeping focus harder and many lose it completely, getting bogged down in trivial activities that won't deliver significant advantages. If you chase too many things at once, you are more than likely to end up with few or no results to show for it. This is where the Bullseye Prioritization strategy comes in very handy. Just as in darts, you focus on the central target, where there's a high pay off, and not the periphery. As you aim for the centre, you're more likely to hit it.

The Bullseye Prioritization strategy invites you to take all your actions, ideas, tasks and interests and, using a bullseye map, spread them across different domains so that only one item stays in the centre. This is vital! When you have that, you place another in the next circle and work outwards. Don't bother going farther than the fourth or fifth circle. I often suggest people stop after the first two and take meaningful action instead. Initially you might find that this exercise takes time as you rearrange items around the bullseye. However, having to choose between activities will help you train your brain in vital decision making about what's truly important to focus on now.

Your bullseye activities might correspond to one day, a week or a longer period. Some people often use the bullseye for planning three months ahead in combination with a twelve-month calendar. When you have an order to your focus, simply apply Strategy 1 (Completion) which is to work towards a tangible goal (stepping stone) that will help you complete that activity. When you arrive at a sensible point with your central task, you can then give attention to the second activity and so on. The bullseye ensures that you no longer split your focus or, worse still, focus your energy on the peripherals. Instead, it forces you to stay with what's key to your success now and focus your whole brain on that.

Bullseye Prioritization strategy questions

- How good are you at always working with your highest priority items instead of peripheral activities on a scale from 1 (poor) to 10 (great)?
- What factors affect the score?
- Are there specific contexts where you prioritize better than others? What makes it that way?

STRATEGY 3: VALUE ADDED RIPPLES

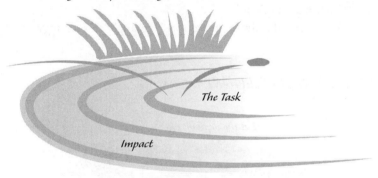

Working with impact through value-added activities

The Task

Impact

Don't aim to be busy, have impact

In a world filled with more and more complex jobs and lack of extra time, it can be easy and tempting to just get on with your work before considering the larger questions about whether it makes sense to do what you do. Value Added Ripples is a critical thinking strategy that reminds the brain to consider how what you do makes a difference, what value it creates and how to optimize what you do for maximal effect to ensure you work smartly. As with the previous strategies, Value Added Ripples can be applied to tasks and people. It might make you think about how to reconnect, rearrange or reposition things to create the desired ripple effect that will amplify your effort and hard work, thus increasing your productivity.

Value Added Ripples strategy questions

- How good are you at considering impact ripples before you take action on a scale from 1 (poor) to 10 (great)?
- What factors affect the score you are at now? What factors would help you increase it?
- Are there specific contexts where you do this more than others? What makes this so?
- Where, specifically, might you wish to apply this strategy now?

STRATEGY 4: BIG ELEPHANT

Eat the elephant piece by piece

Tackle one chunk now !

This is one of the most basic and beloved productivity strategies, which is based on a wise saying about how one eats an elephant – by breaking it down into small pieces.

Anything that is too large to chew in one go needs to be broken down into small, bite-sized chunks. Our brains are the same. They like to deal with information in small bits. The Big Elephant strategy reminds us to break things down, make to-do lists, identify key responsibilities and delegate tasks so that what appears to be a massive undertaking can be completed. Big Elephant might also remind you that big things have massive complexity within them. Think of a real elephant and its anatomical and physiological complexity. It is important to define the level at which you wish to delve in at the start, before risking getting lost in such a big animal.

Big Elephant strategy questions

- How good are you at dividing things up into manageable-sized chunks on a scale from 1 (poor) to 10 (great)?
- What factors affect the score you are at now? How could you increase your score and in which areas/contexts would this be most effective?

STRATEGY 5: PERFECTION BREAK

Mind perfection

*Know when 80% is good enough and when the
last 20% is a 'must' sitting underneath*

High standards are great. They help us to do excellent work that outperforms others and impresses. The results we create say a lot about us, whether it's a company we lead, a product we create, a service we deliver, the food we consume or how we look after others and ourselves. That said, perfection can be a real blocker of productivity. It can hold us captive to a negative mindset where what we do is never good enough.

The Perfection Break strategy is a reminder that the starting point is always a work in progress: a draft. Improvement comes after you have a start product, not before. And one of the biggest obstacles in terms of personal productivity is often the start. The Perfection Break can be applied in many ways and contexts. For instance, when you want to improve what you create and also when you want to give others as well as yourself a break and accept that the work is good enough.

The Perfection Break requires knowledge about what's required, knowledge about what 'good' looks like and the judgement skills to make appropriate decisions for when to continue, and how and when to stop. A good definition of what you aim to achieve at each point, combined with always aiming to do your best within those limits, helps to stop perfectionism from being a paralyzer that can hamper your potential.

Perfection Break strategy questions

- How good are you at judging the level or standard required in the things you attempt on a scale from 1 (poor) to 10 (great)?
- Are there areas where your productivity really suffers from not having a mastery of this strategy?
- What would help you hone your judgement further?

STRATEGY 6: POWER OF OTHERS

Power of others

Use the experience and know-how of others to help you find solutions

Probably the largest obstacle to personal and organizational productivity is people's inability to ask for help from others. I am always amazed by the fear people have of appearing needy, the worry that the feedback might be negative or simply the isolation many people face having no one to ask. Asking for help, advice, a viewpoint or an effective strategy from someone who knows what they are talking about is by far the quickest and most effective strategy for increasing your productivity.

Getting others involved in the work through teams, groups or brainstorms helps to spark innovation and often substantially improves the final product. This is all provided that the people involved are those who have the necessary knowledge and skill to help you. As a strategy, the Power of Others can be used in many creative ways. It can be applied to having honest conversations about difficult issues, problem-solving or idea-generation activities. It can be used to create more effective inductions for new staff at work. It reminds us about an effective use of coaches, mentors, colleagues and friends as well as the power of a kind stranger with a smile on a morning commute. It keeps us grounded and connected with other beings, which is not only effective but also critical for survival. Applying the Power of Others strategy effectively in your work and life will hugely improve your productivity and wellbeing, as well as helping you make wonderful friends and powerful allies.

Power of Others strategy questions

- How good are you at reaching out to others for help on a scale from 1 (poor) to 10 (great)?
- How good are you at making yourself available to help others on a scale from 1 (poor) to 10 (great)?
- What makes it easy to connect with others and what impedes it?
- Are you connecting with the sort of people that can best help you? Do you know who they are?

STRATEGY 7: ENERGY CYCLE

Work with your best energy

Do the hard things at your peak

Are you a morning person or a midnight owl? Or maybe you peak at midday and then suffer an afternoon slump. Most people's productivity varies throughout the day and over a working week. Awareness about when you are at your best is crucial in helping select activities that are well matched to your mood and energy levels for optimal productivity.

Choosing difficult work at a time when you are feeling at your lowest is an easy recipe for failure. This has a double negative effect. Your brain begins to associate failure of starting a task in one state with general failure to be able to get something done at all. Before you know it, the work then ends up being constantly postponed. The Energy Cycle strategy is a powerful reminder to learn about your own peaks and troughs so that you can be more effective. It also means using the knowledge you develop to plan your work and save yourself significant time being unproductive.

Energy Cycle strategy questions

- How good are you at knowing/being aware of your energy levels on a scale from 1 (poor) to 10 (great) in a day or week?

- How will your productivity change if you master this strategy?
- How would you go about that?

STRATEGY 8: POWER OF FIVE

Power of 5 minutes

Put time to good use

A definite top obstacle to getting things done and being and feeling productive is getting started. The Power of Five is a simple and highly effective strategy to get over that barrier. It involves setting a short but definite amount of time (for example, five minutes) for tackling something we are putting off.

The interesting result of using this strategy is that as soon as you delve into the task, you'll often develop the necessary momentum to keep going. As with all the other strategies, the Power of Five can be used in many creative ways. For example, you can use the Power of Five as a reminder to take advantage of short, yet valuable, chunks of time for getting through tasks that can be tackled over that time frame. You can also use it as a motivator for getting started, a time-management technique to put specific time limits on defined activities instead of letting them expand indefinitely. On a most practical and immediate level, the Power of Five can be used to take a few minutes to create simple and helpful to-do lists to give your work structure. I'm sure you will think of many other ways of using the strategy.

Power of Five strategy questions

- How effectively do you use this strategy at the moment on a scale from 1 (not at all) to 10 (frequently)?
- What would be one way that you could begin to introduce this strategy into your work/life to help you raise your productivity?

STRATEGY 9: IT'S UP TO ME

*Be responsible
for your part*

As an individual, you have a tremendous amount of power and control over what you think, feel and do. You have a choice in how you show up and what actions you take.

It's Up to Me is a strategy for exercising personal leadership and being in control of what happens to you. It focuses on identifying root causes of problems where you can act. Many times, you might find you are part of the problem, for example in relationships that are not working out. It's Up to Me should remind you to take personal responsibility for your share of the problem and success. It should then allow you to work from a place of good intentions and an open heart to improve things for others as well as yourself. This strategy speaks to the core of productivity that is achieved when you respect yourself and fully respect others. This respect is a key to achieving holistic productivity, as defined and set out in this book. It's Up to Me is an invitation to be a change maker and a leader: to model good behaviour. See what works and adopt. Spread good practice instead of reinventing the wheel and wasting time. Lead where you must and follow others to generate movement behind their good ideas. All change begins in *you*.

It's Up to Me strategy questions

- How effectively do you use this strategy at the moment on a scale from 1 (not at all) to 10 (frequently)?
- What would be one way that you could begin to introduce this strategy into your work/life to help you raise your productivity?

STRATEGY 10: WORKING WITH FACTS

Work with facts

Gather all key
info at once

One of the key productivity strategies is to work with facts instead of assumptions. Assumptions are highly dangerous. They have no basis in reality and can really confuse our thinking. It is incredible how often individuals, teams and, indeed, whole organizations work in a vacuum, in false realities or lands of make believe. Much of this is shaped by cultures that create conditions for ignorance, insecurity and fear to dominate people's behaviour and ways of working.

Working With Facts is a strategy that will remind you to create the right conditions for examining what truly is, and for adopting the best communication medium to serve this purpose. Imagine the costs of hiring the wrong person – yet many people still choose to interview employees through CVs and poorly designed interviews. Think of a group of people trying to pin down a meeting over email instead of electronic meeting schedulers. Many such activities stem from ignorance and poor choices, waste valuable time, cost money and are hugely unproductive; likewise conflict, interpersonal turf wars, personal agendas and a whole list of other misdemeanours that take energy away from results into the wasteland of total lack of productivity.

Working With Facts offers many possibilities. It can help improve team meetings, one-to-one discussions and help with larger planning and strategy creation activities. It helps people to feel involved and engaged. It can also help individuals become more productive on their own by reminding them to check their facts before jumping to conclusions and actions that will not create the desired results. Considering how you communicate, when and to what purpose is a critical strategy for success and probably the hardest to master, as it involves working with other people and continuously adopting and developing your style for best results.

Working with Facts strategy questions

- How effectively do you communicate at the moment on a scale from 1 (poor) to 10 (very good)? You may wish to consider different communication media in turn.
- What stops you from adopting more effective communication methods in your key interactions or work projects?
- What steps can you take to improve?

STRATEGY 11: PLANNING

Planning saves time doing

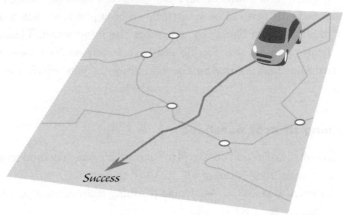

Success

Good plans help to avoid chaos

Perhaps the oldest and simplest productivity strategy for achieving amazing results is planning. This strategy can include everything from the humble to-do list, formalized project management approaches such as Price2, to visualization techniques that allow you to imagine or envisage the outcome in its full complexity.

Whether the task is small or enormous, creating a plan for what will be done, who will do it, when, how and why is critical to productivity because it saves valuable time. You probably try to do much of this already. The key with using planning well on a small scale is to list activities that are expressed in task form (something you can do) and which can therefore be achieved.

Often, the tendency is to list tasks that are indeed whole projects. This is counter-productive and demotivating, as it is nearly always impossible to get them done in one go. This means that assessing progress becomes difficult. Think about what happens to you when you set yourself a massive task that, in fact, is a whole project. Large projects require many tasks. They might have specific sequences. To maintain progress and feel a sense of momentum, you need to work with a list of subtasks, not just the project. Planning through a simple to-do list that can be written down on a phone or sketchpad frees the brain from having to remember the information. This, in turn, helps to ensure that you do not have to rely on your memory and that your brain is free to concentrate on actions which create results.

Planning strategy questions

- To what extent do you use planning to help you stay productive on a scale from 1 (not at all) to 10 (frequently)?
- In which areas of your life would planning really create a positive difference for you?

STRATEGY 12: BINS

Bins are made for a reason!

*Time spent doing the wrong
things is still wasted time*

All activities benefit from a periodic review in order to decide whether the activity is worth pursuing or if it is no longer needed in its current form and can be binned. Some tasks and work no longer need to be done. Some become obsolete or lose priority over more critical actions. Some need to be reviewed and possibly reconsidered.

Bins is a strategy that is often overlooked when you get very busy. When you become so immersed in activities that you can't find a moment to look above the horizon line, you risk losing focus, going off on unhelpful tangents and losing valuable time.

The Bins strategy can be applied to everything from work to daily life. In effect, it is a decluttering strategy. As time moves and things change, including yourself, Bins is a way to make space and time for new developments, careers and projects as well as relationships and hobbies. As such, Bins is also a strategy to help maintain your happiness and satisfaction on a regular basis.

Bins strategy questions

- How frequently do you review what needs binning in your work and life on a scale from 1 (not at all) to 10 (frequently)?
- What would be the biggest benefit for you if you used this strategy on a regular basis?
- Where would be the best place to start?

STRATEGY 13: LYNCHPINS

Crack the key problem

Don't aim to be busy, have impact

The last strategy is a key to all productivity and that's the lynchpin – identifying the key problem or root cause. Often, productivity suffers because you may be working on the periphery of the problem, or you may be absorbed by activities that, while urgent or worth doing, are not going to move you as far forward as tackling the key area. In communication this means talking about surface stuff instead of exploring deeper emotional content that strengthens relationships and creates real interpersonal bonds.

The Lynchpin strategy helps you to really think about what you are focusing and/or working on and why. It will remind you that being busy is not the same as being productive. Productivity is not simply about speed. It is about making time count in all areas, creating the right sort of ripples and achieving inspiring results. The Lynchpin should also remind you about using the right tool to crack the problem. A combination of focused effort and the right tools will help ensure that you get the right things done in the least amount of time.

Lynchpins strategy questions

- To what extent do you focus on identifying the lynchpins in your work and life on a scale from 1 (not at all) to 10 (frequently)?
- To what extent do you feel you have a sufficiently rich toolbox of skills, experiences and contacts to help you be productive?
- What is missing most and how could you acquire it?

GET PRODUCTIVE STRATEGIES EXERCISE

1. Take each of the thirteen productivity strategies and brainstorm as many ideas from each one as you can imagine for applying each strategy in your life and/or work. The more lateral connections you can make for each strategy, the better. Aim for at least five. You're doing well if you can think of ten.

Notes:

2. Go through your strategies and highlight any ideas that you can definitely use or apply in your life right now. Make a plan to show how you will do this.

Illustrative examples:

Crack the key problem

Don't aim to be busy, have impact

- Ask my customers what they most value about my service.
- Talk to my boss about my career prospects within the company.
- Complete my qualification exam.
- Write a letter explaining my position and ask for a meeting to follow up.
- Invite an expert to assess our IT requirements.
- Study our key competitors and identify our differentiation edge.

- Come up with one specific employee reward that aligns with our company values.
- Give things more time to unfold before taking action.
- Say what's on my mind.

Work with your best energy

Do the hard things at your peak

- Do two house chores in the morning before work.
- Use the end of the day to plan my key activities for tomorrow.
- Remember that tiredness is normal and do not stress about it.
- Spend thirty minutes of my peak time coming up with solutions to our key problems.
- Alternate team meetings between morning, midday and afternoon.
- Schedule meetings with X first thing on Monday.
- Figure out when my project manager is at his or her peak.
- Introduce an energy-mapping exercise into a brainstorming session to work more effectively with the group.
- Identify natural pick-me-uppers for late afternoon in the office.

THIRTEEN PROVEN PRODUCTIVITY STRATEGIES YOU NEED TO KNOW: TAKEAWAY LESSONS

You made it. You have acquainted yourself with, or refreshed your knowledge of, thirteen general strategies that will improve your productivity. Hopefully, as you worked through each set of strategy questions, you also developed awareness about the strategies you use often and those you might not be using very much at this stage. You also might have discovered that, while you can be very creative in how you interpret each strategy, and that's very important for helping you to be productive, some strategies will naturally fit and match your situation more directly. This is what we want. If you master this material well, you will easily be able to pick strategies relevant to any problem you face and then use them in combinations that will help you get good results.

26

DEVELOP PRODUCTIVE THINKING

The following Get Productive Thinking exercise is a systematic productivity enhancing technique. It is based on the simple and practical strategies you discovered in the previous chapter, which can be creatively adopted and combined into an individual action plan that suits you and your specific context. By focusing on what you wish to produce and/or create, you can select the key strategy or combination of strategies that matches what's needed in that instant for you. This means that you have a series of specific, unique steps or a single step to achieving what you want.

Where you put your focus affects the results you achieve. Focus on the end goal, not the intermediates, when you consider intermediate action. Focusing on what doesn't work (the blockers) tends to draw you back to a negative space. A far more effective method is to focus on what you want, because the linkage of positive outcomes with positive emotions in your brain immediately gives you more constructive alternatives. This will help you to behave in a mature and professional manner and will yield amazing outcomes; it is not easy, but it is what is required for high-level productivity.

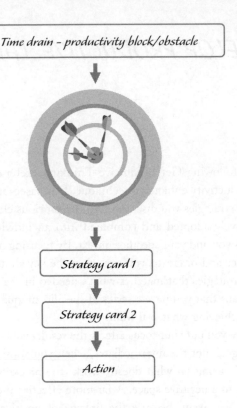

Time drain - productivity block/obstacle

Strategy card 1

Strategy card 2

Action

1. Rephrase a problem, challenge or obstacle into a positive, specific statement of what you would like to have.

Notes:

2. Pick strategies or a strategy that come to your mind or use those covered in this section. What's key is that the strategies you pick directly help you achieve the results you want in your opinion.

Notes:

3. If you have more than one strategy to get to your result, arrange your strategies into a logical sequence of steps. Aim for a minimum number of steps and omit obvious steps.

4. Take action according to your plan.

Example 1

Productivity barrier: attempting too much.
Positive goal: get substantial amount done on one key task.
Strategy:

1. Lynchpins (13) – focus on the one item I want to do today.
2. Completion (1) – define specific milestones that will mark progress for today's work.
3. Big Elephant (4) – break up work into small bites and write them down with a tick box window that I can mark as I complete each one.

Action:
Notes:

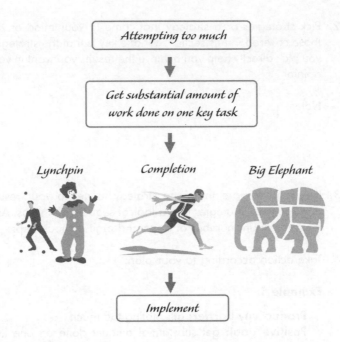

A different person may choose different strategies, but even with the same set and order of strategies, their strategy storyline will be completely different, as illustrated by Example 2.

Example 2

Productivity barrier: attempting too much.
Positive goal: get substantial amount done on one key task.
Strategy:

1. Lynchpins (13) – speak to Mark about how to proceed.
2. Completion (1) – define what success will look like exactly.
3. Big Elephant (4) – write a day-by-day plan of the work.

Action:
Notes:

 DEVELOP PRODUCTIVE THINKING:
TAKEAWAY LESSONS

As I hope you have noticed from working through your own examples, the key to tackling your productivity barrier is to start with a picture of a desired result. Therefore, the first step after you name your productivity block is to convert it into what you do want! A useful question to ask yourself is: *What would exist or what would be happening if the block did not exist?*

Your exact strategy will be unique to you. No one else can tell you how you should go about it, as they are not you. So trust yourself. Your brain will tell you what it thinks is a good starting point. But suppose that you carry out your series of steps and still don't achieve what you want or that you get stuck on one of your steps. That's great. You have just learned valuable information about what you might still be missing, or where you're encountering a new hurdle you didn't predict. This means you can adjust your strategy to account for that until you get what you want. At some point, you will be able to do all of this in your head the way you already use some of the strategies, or a version of them, to good effect.

27

DEVELOP PRODUCTIVE CONVERSATIONS

Conversations are fundamental to productivity, whether that's getting results, finding out information, creating a partnership, building a productive team or indeed a company. They are vital in good customer service to clients and for problem solving when things go wrong. And yet, sometimes, very little time seems to be invested in preparing for conversations to go well. Very little time is spent on setting out the goals of a conversation or thinking about how you want to be in a conversation, as well as how you want the other person to feel during and after the conversation. Instead, more often than not, there is a tendency to jump straight into conversations rather casually, unless the conversation or meeting is perceived to be difficult. This is a poor approach. If you don't plan, there is no reference point. Without a goal it can be easy to get lost and you may fail to achieve what you set out to achieve in your interactions with somebody.

The Get Productive Communication exercise is a framework that is based on general productivity strategies you will be discovering in this section, as well as something far more basic: respect for others. When we communicate with respect we value the other person instead of being selfish and only worrying about ourselves. We remain polite, we listen, we test our comprehension, we find out their point of view through inquiry, we seek to understand and build common ground, we empathize, we invite honesty and own what is ours (fears, practicalities and so on). We don't play games or try to control what the other person says. Instead, we focus on the end goal – a productive interaction – and we gauge how we're doing through regular feedback.

Conversations, by their very nature, involve teamwork. Two or more people carry responsibility for their success and failure. If we make mistakes we apologize. If we run out of ideas, we ask for help early on instead of waiting for situations to get worse. Productive conversations require an investment. We invest trust, openness and courage and we leave our ego outside the room. This does not mean you have to take ages in all interactions. Indeed being able to manage your time is a sign of respect for your own productivity and that of the other person. It simply means that there is no place in a conversation to dwell on who is right and who is wrong, or who is to blame. This way of being and behaving creates winners and losers and no one likes to lose. In productive conversations everybody wins. In the exercise that follows you will develop your own framework for having productive conversations and a way to track your progress. We all get things wrong from time to time. Your aim is not to be perfect! It is to learn and continuously improve.

GET PRODUCTIVE COMMUNICATION EXERCISE

1. Think of a recent conversation, either with one other person or perhaps a meeting you held. Note down to what extent you valued/appreciated/respected the other person/people on a scale of 1 (not at all) to 10 (very much). If the score is low, think about something you can find to appreciate about them now. If you are stuck, look for similarities between yourself and the other person/people.

   Notes:

2. Write down what you wanted to achieve. What was your goal for this conversation?

   Notes:

3. The table below contains thirteen productivity strategies with possible examples to get you started. These are illustrative. Go through each strategy and come up with a way to apply this strategy in your conversation. Your goal is to generate options.

Productivity Strategy	Example: Application in Productive Conversation	You
Completion (1)	Define a clear goal.	
Bullseye prioritization (2)	Get clear on the one thing that must be achieved.	
Value added ripples (3)	Longer-term impact of a productive conversation.	
Big elephant (4)	Apart from what is discussed, what else is at stake?	
Perfection break (5)	I'm going to focus on being clear, not being nervous.	
Power of others (6)	I will thank the other person for making time to see me.	
Energy cycle (7)	Let's schedule this for midday.	
Power of five (8)	Let's give us a specific timeframe.	
It's up to me (9)	I'm going to actively listen.	
Working with facts (10)	I will bring along last month's performance figures.	
Planning (11)	I will ask/suggest items for discussion ahead of the meeting.	
Bins (12)	What I don't want to talk about.	

(Continued)

Productivity Strategy	Example: Application in Productive Conversation	You
Lynchpins (13)	No matter what, I will always respect the other person's right to their opinion.	

4. Looking at the thirteen strategies and your own ways of using them, pick those that would be most useful for you here.

 Reflective Questions

- Are you truly open to discovering and learning about the other person's perspective, especially when it might be different from yours?
- How do you normally review the success of your conversations? Do you make a point of asking for feedback? How do you give positive feedback about what worked for you? How would doing these things benefit you and the other person or people?
- Given the strategies above, what comes easy to you and what do you find you need to pay more attention to in conversations?

 DEVELOP PRODUCTIVE CONVERSATIONS: TAKEAWAY LESSONS

We are almost always in conversation and, maybe because we tend to spend our early years mastering how to talk and the meaning of words, we develop a false sense of security that, by the time we are adults, we should be good at conversations. This is a very large assumption to make. Regular practice does not make us good.

Purposeful practice does. I hope that, as you become familiar with the productive strategies, you will develop the habit of being purposeful in your conversations. By starting with true respect and appreciation for the other person, you will hopefully be able to keep a free and open heart and mind. This may feel arduous with some people, but the more you practise the better you will get.

With time you will be able to plan and hold a full repertoire of your own effective practices for various conversations – from seemingly trivial to those with higher stakes – and leaving less to chance. The more you practise how you approach and hold conversations, the more productive your conversations will become. This will save you lots of time in the short and long term. When you respect others, you give the necessary time to create the right outcome. There is always a purpose to what you say and how you say it. Making this aim explicit for yourself before you begin is a great habit to develop. It prevents sloppiness that can easily spiral into misunderstanding. Take responsibility for your half of the conversation. Stay true to the larger purpose and avoid getting caught in unproductive dialogue. If you feel the conversation is taking a bad turn, acknowledge what you see or, if necessary, take time out. Be at peace so that you can be respectful.

28

ASK PRODUCTIVE QUESTIONS

The strategies mentioned in this section are proven and useful. Applying them in your life in a way that fits your context on a regular basis will definitely help you achieve more in less time. However, it's possible to plan, prioritize, envisage and even bin activities but still not make the most of time. To take things to the next level, what you need to do is ask productive questions. Most of the time, when you are swamped with lots to do, you react to what is happening instead of really thinking about it. Asking questions that help you find the thread of the problem or challenge so that you work on the root causes and can create a systemic positive change is key to good productivity.

Being able to step away and find the discipline of using your brain to think and unravel the apparent complexity, instead of just rolling up your sleeves and jumping in, can be challenging and even counter-intuitive action for some people. The following exercise will help you develop your thinking in a similar way to how highly productive individuals think.

FINDING THE THREAD EXERCISE

1. Pick a situation you want to explore in detail to identify a possible way forward. For example: getting promoted.

2. Now go through the thirteen productivity strategies below and formulate one to three questions you could ask about your situation.Below are some examples to help you get started.

Productivity Strategy	Productive Questions
Completion (1)	What do I really want? And what else? What will success look like?
Bullseye prioritization (2)	What is most important here? What have I forgotten that's key?
Value added ripples (3)	How can profits be maximized? Who else will be affected by this decision?

(Continued)

Productivity Strategy	Productive Questions
Big elephant (4)	Is this elephant worth working on? Is there demand for this product? How can we make this massive initiative attractive to our volunteers?
Perfection break (5)	Where do we need to excel? What can we outsource?
Power of others (6)	Who do we need on our team? Who can help me most?
Energy cycle (7)	Is this the right time for a launch? What rewards can be offered to staff members to help them stay motivated?
Power of five (8)	What can be done right now? What are the quick wins? How can this be done more efficiently?
It's up to me (9)	What am I taking responsibility for? Can we talk about this?
Working with facts (10)	What are we not able to see? How did we get this wrong and what do we need to do to prevent similar errors? What other contrary evidence exists?
Planning (11)	What does our plan look like? How can we do this with less? Is everyone clear about what we are doing and why?

Productivity Strategy	Productive Questions
Bins (12)	What can be abandoned? How can costs be saved without jeopardizing the quality of the product? Where does our waste really go?
Lynchpins (13)	What is the big challenge? What would an ideal solution look like? Can I just say what I really mean?

3. When you have a list of questions, go through and answer each one as honestly as you can. If further questions suggest themselves, answer them too. Aim to explore as much of the situation as you can until you find a thread of a solution.

 Reflective Questions

- Are you more interested in creating quick results or getting to the bottom of a problem by exploring it in detail? How does your focus influence the final outcome? What biases are likely to exist?
- What methods could you use to collect additional perspectives and ideas to help you understand the situation more fully?
- Given the strategies above, which strategies come easy to you and what do you tend to omit? What would be the immediate benefit of using more productive questions in your life and at work?
- What tends to stop you from asking productive questions when they are in your head? How can you ask the question without feeling at risk?
- If you consider 'what' and 'how' questions, is there a difference between them? Is one type more effective than the other in some situations?

ASK PRODUCTIVE QUESTIONS: TAKEAWAY LESSONS

In many situations at work and in life, asking certain questions can be associated with being difficult or negative. Many people fear asking questions altogether. This tends to kill productivity, stifle the expression of honest views and therefore ruin any chance of a common understanding of the situation being shared among the group of people working together. Refraining from asking questions can result in a lot of wasted effort and resources, as well as people having trouble being fully engaged and/or confusion. Developing a culture where you can ask productive questions is fundamental to high performance and getting things done. Productive questions open doors to key information, insights and perspectives that are not just valuable but critical. They help you understand what is going on in full so that your brain can set to work on finding the best solutions and generating useful ideas. If you are missing key information, your brain will be solving the wrong problem.

Coming up with a productive question is your responsibility if you're going to get things done well and succeed. Trust your gut. Most of the time, people have great questions to ask but worry about looking foolish. Don't let this worry you. Treat everything you do as if it was yours, because it is. Even if you work for someone else, what you do and how well you do it reflects who you are. Stay engaged and you will enjoy your work more. Be curious and follow the thread or threads of a problem or challenge you are passionate about. And if you lose your passion, get curious about that too. When you do explore it, you will be rewarded with clarity and a solution that makes sense, solves the problem at the root level and feels satisfying.

SECTION FIVE

GET IN THE ZONE AND MAKE TIME COUNT

I can tell you that being in the zone feels great! It keeps things interesting. This book will, hopefully, prove to be a big step on your journey to that zone. Getting into the zone and staying there is about making time count every minute, day after day. It's about clarifying and living your purpose – the life you were meant to live – while being the best version of you. This is the ultimate in personal productivity and is fundamental for building effective teams, businesses and organizations. It is a journey of continuous development in which you deepen your self-knowledge through reflection, think for yourself, act in accordance with your needs and develop skills to relate to others with the same level of love and respect you deserve. Getting in the zone is a key step for effective leadership and is, in my view, fundamental to effective development programmes. Being in the zone relies on being true to yourself, having the courage to let your dreams, skills and aspirations take centre stage, thinking big and taking responsibility for what you do and create. People in the zone truly come alive and create powerful results because there is a complete alignment between their energy, ability and action. Whether you already know what you want to achieve or are still formulating your plans, the exercises in this section will help you distil your purpose and clarify your interests and aspirations.

29

TAKE CONTROL OF THE IMPACT YOU MAKE

Our sheer presence gives us an impact. We have impact with our words and our deeds as well as what we choose not to say or do. What you do, say and how you behave affects you as well as everything around you. This gives you lots of power for good as well as for damage. You can be helpful or you can be a block to yourself and others. You can love or you can choose to be at war with yourself and/or others. It's all a choice and you're the decision maker.

In the exercise that follows, you will have an opportunity to map out the various areas, communities, groups and teams where you show up on a regular basis to help you assess your impact on them and their impact on you. The exercise will highlight where you are potentially reacting as opposed to actively choosing the impact you make, where you might be sitting on the fence and giving up your control to shape the results even though you have the power to do so through your voice and your presence. It might highlight areas where you feel isolated and help you to consider and address the reasons for this, which might be preventing you from being your best. The exercise aims to help you become a powerful, conscious decision maker and shaper of results. This will not only improve your productivity but will also raise the overall productivity of these groups.

PERSONAL IMPACT MAP EXERCISE

1. Using the following schematic as a guide, sketch out various communities, teams, institutions and groups (including family and interpersonal relationships) of which you are a part or which you might be leading. You may choose to label each circle as shown below.

2. Notice the complexity of your map and the variety of roles you play in different circles. Note the role(s) you play in each circle. For example, you might be a leader, member, facilitator, advisor, friend, participant, etc. Take a moment to appreciate what the different hats you wear require of you. You may wish to note down what comes easily and what you find more challenging.

Notes:

3. Assess your impact in each role. Is the impact you make in line with your expectations? What is your aim? For example, are you making the difference you want to make, are you being seen, are you trusted to lead, are you appreciated for your knowledge and expertise? If not, note what you can do to increase your impact generally.

Notes:

4. Take note of the skills, behaviours and immense knowledge you must have. Note also anything that you may need to develop, such as leadership, negotiation, courage, confidence, appreciation, cultural sensitivity and so on.

Notes:

Boosting your impact

1. For each circle where you want to maximize your impact, what would real productivity look like there? What do you contribute and what's truly stopping you from creating better results?

   Notes:

2. What and/or who is most important in each circle? Who do you need to get on board, join with, influence? How can you go about this?

   Notes:

 Reflective Questions

- Is your impact in line with what you hope to achieve in each role? Is your impact in line with the sort of person you want to be?
- How does each circle impact upon you? How does it make you feel; what does it make you think or do?
- Are there others with good ideas/efforts that might really benefit from your support?

- What actions will you take to change the impact you have or the impact you experience? Aim for one key action that will greatly improve the group's impact or your impact in that circle.

 ## TAKE CONTROL OF THE IMPACT YOU MAKE: TAKEAWAY LESSONS

The Personal Impact Map exercise is a very powerful method for analyzing your actions and behaviours and their effect on the outcomes. I have used this exercise with teams, organizational leaders and individuals looking at advancing their position and career as well as with those wishing to improve their interpersonal relationships. Hopefully, you will have gained new awareness about your existing and possible productivity in various circles that will help you to make concrete choices about how you want to behave and be in each area. You might become aware of things you're doing in some areas that directly create positive results, which you may want to adapt to other circles. You may notice an apparent need to withdraw from some areas or a need to join new ones. With some reflection and an action plan, you will be reviewing and consistently improving your impact across all key areas where you show up, and that's the goal of this exercise.

30
IDENTIFY HOW YOU ADD VALUE

E ach of us has many opportunities to make a positive difference, to add value to other people's experience, to our work places, businesses, individuals, communities and indeed to the world we live in. Each of us can be a change maker. Personal productivity, and indeed organizational productivity, is linked to the frequency and scale of positive changes you can make on a regular basis within the sphere of influence you are given or which you can create.

The exercise that follows will help you to build your own positive change maker CV and analyze the trend. Completing this exercise will raise your awareness of the skills you use to make a positive difference and will help you to identify specific conditions that bring this out in you. Knowing this will help you to make an even larger difference to the spheres around you.

POSITIVE DIFFERENCE TRAJECTORY EXERCISE

1. The following diagram represents a trajectory of the positive difference you have made up to this point, starting with your birth. The positive differences are demarcated with smiley faces. Note down smileys you actively created with your actions through time. You may choose to be creative and use stickers to mark positive differences you have made. You might decide to make ticks. Your goal is to create a broad map of how productive you have been so far.

Your birth	+10 years	+10 years	+10 years	+10 years
Skills you learned, displayed, used in making a positive difference at each stage				

2. Now let's delve deeper. Note down clearly what you did and who benefited from your actions. You may wish to do this in two columns. On the left, write down what you did and on

the right, the impact and who benefited. If you benefited too, note this down.

Notes:

3. Have a look through the people who benefit most from your efforts. Who are they? What characteristics do they all share? What is it that you really do for them?

Notes:

4. Come up with a sentence that can summarize the positive difference you make and to what sort of people. For example: 'I help other social entrepreneurs start their movements' or 'I lend my creative thinking to people who look for better solutions' or 'I use my criticism to help people improve what they do.'

Notes:

Reflective Questions

- How does your trajectory look so far in terms of the positive difference you have made up to the present moment? Does it grow or decline? Does it allow you to see where you will be in the next ten years? Twenty years? How does it make you feel about yourself?
- What allowed you to make the positive difference at each stage?
- What special skills do you have to make a difference or what skills are you especially good at using? What skills have you added? What skills (if any) have you lost along the way?
- Given your skills and impact so far, where else or with whom do you stand to make a positive difference?

IDENTIFY HOW YOU ADD VALUE: TAKEAWAY LESSONS

The Positive Difference Trajectory exercise is rich in useful information. What you discover ought to make you feel proud and help inspire you to further greatness. You ought to be more aware of the qualities and skills the exercise highlighted for you in which you excel and those you may wish to develop either on your own or with someone else. The knowledge you have gained might also give you clues about how you might grow your influence in the future and ideas about specific arenas for doing this. As you bring more conscious awareness to your activities and aim to make an ever larger positive difference, your sense of productivity and satisfaction will grow.

31

UNCOVER YOUR SPECIFIC AND UNIQUE CAPABILITIES

We are walking assemblages of our experiences, skills, talents and backgrounds. This creates a complex and valuable world of individual relatedness through similarities as well as individual uniqueness. The similarities we can identify between others and ourselves provide common ground for collective achievement and collaboration. Our uniqueness, in turn, allows for individual contribution and a sense of personal stake in the things we do.

Your talents, skills, wisdom, insights and experiences are gifts that you can tap into to enhance your creativity and problem solving, to give you ideas about potential career choices and to inspire you when you feel stuck. They can also be sources of ideas for services and businesses.

Often people fall into the trap of defining themselves through their key activities or roles. So, for example, this might be the job you are currently doing or the role you hold, such as a manager, CEO, receptionist, etc. However, this is highly limiting for your thinking and how others will perceive you. There is even a term for this – *pigeonholing* people.

It's about time you began to see yourself as more than just what you do right now. The Mighty Gifts Hunt is an excellent exercise to help you get out of your pigeonhole and examine the wealth of gifts you carry in a systematic fashion, by looking at both what you can do and how you go about doing it. It will help you notice the skills you may have forgotten, abilities you might be taking for granted. It should also inspire you with ideas for developing your skills further. The work you do here will support your ongoing productivity in an ever-changing world.

MIGHTY GIFTS HUNT EXERCISE

1. Make a list of your key experiences, knowledge and skills/abilities from everything you have done up to now (paid or unpaid). You may wish to capture them in three lists, as shown below, three columns or with a spider or mind-mapping diagram. Choose a method that works best for you.

   Example

   Experiences (things that have happened to you):

   - Moving home every two years and having to learn a new language.
   - Losing a parent and having to look after younger siblings.
   - Winning a major prize.

   Knowledge (things you know well or extremely well):

   - Subject expert in specific field and/or degree holder.
   - Hold lots of knowledge about key competitor.
   - Know how social networking works.

   Skills/Abilities (things you can do yourself):

   - Create a good presentation in PowerPoint.
   - Negotiate the best deal.
   - Save impressive amounts of money on grocery bills.

2. Note down specific aspects of your upbringing, culture, particular circumstances and any other characteristics that make up your experience to date. This might help you identify things that you might have missed or omitted above. For example, your nationality, the fact that you got started in work at an early age, that you raised your kids alone or overcame a major disability, etc.

Notes:

3. Think of the items on your list as the 'Whats'. Next to each one write down a brief 'How to' you could share if you were to impart what you know to others. Don't be shy about it or self-critical. Your list might include things like how to effectively move home, find a dream job, have a successful relationship, build an effective team, get fit, make a good trade or lasagne. The list should really exhaust you. It might take pages. Your goal is to capture all the relevant information you can use to draw on to identify your gifts and talents.

4. Now look through your list and notes and write down key skills you displayed in each case. For example: developing agreement, writing, team-building, designing, generating useful ideas, etc. You can write them out as one long string with commas. If skills repeat, that's good. Note them each time they come up. When you finish, go through your string and count the most frequent words. Turn these into a skills list.

What?	How?	Key Skills
Got a major promotion.	1. Identified a key challenge at work and a new post with responsibility to address it.	Can horizon scan for key challenges.
	2. Spoke with a selection of senior managers to sound out their views about the gap and the benefits of solving this problem for the business.	Can put together a short business case and an effective pitch.
	3. Met with the director and pitched the role and myself for it.	Confident to speak with superiors with respect as a valuable colleague.

5. Looking at your key skills, what would you say are your major talents or your one specific talent? Do you perhaps have a knack for building relationships or generating results or solving problems? Note down your talents, as these are your mighty gifts.

Notes:

6. Thinking about your mighty gifts or gift, write down ideas for what you could do given your talent. Your goal is to list as many ideas as you can conceive. They are just ideas. When you finish, go through your list and mark those that attract your energy. How could you create a means of doing what attracts you in your existing job or life?

Notes:

 Reflective Questions

- Where are you an expert? Perhaps you're a natural learner, fixer, problem solver, strategist or visionary. Perhaps you have a knack for engaging people or selling. Perhaps you have a presence that relaxes others or inspires them. Aim to capture all the things you do well, as these are your talents.

- Where else could your talent(s) be applied? Who would benefit and how? What skills can your talents be developed into that capture your interest?
- Which skills could be turned into a product or service? Don't give this too much time. If answers appear quickly, fine. If not, skip it and move on. The key point here is to get your mind to think about natural applications of your skills and talents and increase your awareness of the possibilities. Things you want to do and areas where you identify opportunities you wish to follow up will emerge naturally.
- What action does the information you generated in this exercise inspire in you?

UNCOVER YOUR SPECIFIC AND UNIQUE CAPABILITIES: TAKEAWAY LESSONS

When completed, this exercise should help you collect and recognize lots of characteristics, attributes and capabilities that you have amassed up to now. It will help you appreciate how your unique combination of experiences, talents and skills has morphed into a very special unit – you! This is your offering. No one else will ever be like you. The world is very large and for every person who knows how to do something, there might be many others who desire the same information, a specific product or solution. For every person there is a perfect fit, whether that's a specific place of work, people, challenge or need. Make sure you find yours so that you can play to your strengths and shine.

Completing this exercise might have given you ideas for further possibilities to employ your expertise and experience. Perhaps you got an idea for a new service or business. You might be motivated to connect with others with similar skills, backgrounds or interests. The Mighty Gifts Hunt should help you develop a language for selling your skills to others. This is crucial in career management, at interviews and in developing working collaborations. People are always interested in what you have to offer and whether they can use it.

Finally, by systematically examining your specific gifts, you will be able to develop your talents and skills more purposefully. When you know what you want to achieve or the sort of people you want to work with, you can work out the critical steps you need to take to make this happen. Targeted, continuous development and learning are fundamental to productivity. In today's world that requires fast and productive thinking; being able to draw on all of your experiences to inspire effective solutions will help you become someone people respect, value and want to work with.

32

GET RESULTS THAT ARE WORTH THE EFFORT

Ultimate productivity is about getting results that are worth the effort and that enrich you and the world around you. In business this might mean sustainability and corporate social responsibility. On a personal level, this is about inner satisfaction and a sense of control.

Being productive is mostly about utilizing the energy within you to take purposeful action instead of doing nothing. Many people have a lot of things in their mind that they would like to get done. For some, the list can be so long that it becomes difficult to find the energy to make a start.

Some people struggle to make a decision about *how* to start or what to do *first*. If this has ever happened to you, no doubt you experienced a feeling of confusion or felt overwhelmed. Perhaps it caused you to feel stressed and anxious. Feeling overwhelmed is one of the top reasons people seek help with their time management when, in fact, the underlying cause of their lack of productivity often turns out to be a lack of clarity about priorities. In the sea of possibilities and long to-do lists, developing a sense of clarity about what to do and a certainty about why what you're doing is worthwhile, is key to maintaining high-level productivity.

The Action Funnel is a great method for developing action that has a clear purpose which will resonate with you and inspire the necessary drive. It is based on the principle of energy that attracts us to the things we really want to do because they clearly move us forward and generate desired results. The funnel will help you to consider what you are doing in the present and whether this is likely to produce what you want. When this checks out, you should have more certainty and motivation to act. If your action is not likely to produce what you want, the resulting feedback loop can help you to adjust your actions accordingly. The Action Funnel will help you to systematically make logical adjustments to what you're doing or help generate new alternatives that can save valuable time which would otherwise be misdirected on impossible outcomes.

ACTION FUNNEL EXERCISE

1. Imagine each ball in the diagram below corresponds to a specific activity you are doing at the moment. You may wish to pick a specific time frame for this exercise that suits your context and needs – for example, one week, a month or the last six months.

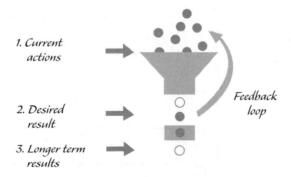

1. *Current actions*

2. *Desired result*

3. *Longer term results*

Feedback loop

2. Write out all the things you are doing at the moment that would be the action balls going into the funnel of desired outcomes.

Notes:

3. Take a look at each ball in turn. Based on the action you have either taken or are taking, are you on course to achieve the outcome you want? If not, note down the adjustments you need to make to what you're doing as your feedback loop.

Action	On course to achieve outcome?	Adjustments to make

4. Once you adjust your existing actions through the feedback loop, consider the longer term consequences of the results you are creating. Write down where you think these results will take you in a year, two years, five years. Is this consistent with what you want in the longer term?

Notes:

 Reflective Questions

- What do your longer term goals (the things at the bottom of the funnel) say about what you want to achieve at the moment and what's important in your life?
- What activities will produce the long-term results that you most desire right now? How can you ensure you prioritize them appropriately?
- Which activities would you group together because they all contribute towards similar long-term goals?
- Which activities (if any) might need to be dropped or postponed? Which balls at the top of the funnel need not come into it at all?

GET RESULTS THAT ARE WORTH THE EFFORT: TAKEAWAY LESSONS

If you did the Action Funnel exercise well, you ought to have a good grasp of the outcomes you want, what your current actions are producing for you and where your efforts are taking you in the longer term. This means you can really step back and evaluate whether what you're doing today is the most effective way of creating what you want. Often, when I work with clients, we find this is not the case. The Action Funnel is good at highlighting what needs to change.

The Action Funnel might help you eliminate tasks that are not helping you move in the right direction or at the right speed. This is good. It will allow you to refocus on those activities that do and take more responsibility for creating results you feel excited about. The Action Funnel often helps individuals get away from being trapped in a busy, yet not hugely productive, state, developing or reinforcing commitment to take action and building the drive to continue, as it clearly shows you that, apart from the unpredictable, it is you and only you that gets to shape your future by what you do today.

33

HONE YOUR KEY MESSAGE(S)

To get things done we communicate. We talk about, consider and evaluate the importance of an idea or task, its relevance, the way it may impact and/or inspire others and ourselves. We discuss our thinking and plans. And we often talk about the how. Communication is a proven way of working up ideas and engaging with the world around us. The world and others give our ideas legs, make us believe, improve our thinking and tell us to keep going or to stop.

Given the importance of communication, it is not surprising that most people can still improve how they communicate with others as well as with themselves for best results. The Key Message exercise will help you to hone in on your message, be it a philosophy of being, how to tell someone what you need and what's not working or how to inspire others or yourself to action. It should help you to develop a good quality message that is well considered and permeated with a pure intention.

Given that communication is vital for productivity, this exercise is truly worth your time. Repeat it often – when you're excited, when you're angry, when you really struggle with what's going on inside you and when you can't wait to tell the world your thoughts. With time you will develop confidence and trust that whatever you're thinking, well-formulated and considered thoughts are worth sharing.

KEY MESSAGE EXERCISE

1. Your task is to convey a message that you truly care about to a specific audience of your choice. It could be a single person, a specific team or another group of people. It could be all of humanity. This is your opportunity to share your message with the world. Something you truly care about or want others to know or pay attention to.

2. What is your actual message? Note down three to five key points that you wish to get across first. Once you have those, think about and write down how your points could be expressed in a single sentence. What's the common trend, underlying main point or call to action contained within it?

Notes:

Be productive:
choose to make a difference!

3. Now think about where the desire for your message has come from within you. Write down what emotions/events have inspired this. Why is this message important for you? If you have more than one key message, do this for each one and see whether your messages are linked or share a common origin.

Notes:

4. Note down what you want to achieve with your message. Do you wish to inspire, criticize, excite, enthuse, offer hope or achieve something else entirely? Note down your key audience.

Notes:

5. What do you need to do/say to capture your audience's attention? Note down the best medium/media you could use to deliver your message. For example, your message could end up on a recording, a large display board or in a newspaper ad. It could be a talk, a seminar or a book.

Notes:

6. How will you package your message so that your audience hears you? How will you know they did hear you? Will you need others to help you deliver it? You may wish to think about key opinion leaders, champions or individuals with access to and/or influence over your key audience. If so, who would be good? Note down any specific names or ideas.

Notes:

Reflective Questions

- What messages are you aware of around you? These could be messages at work, in your surroundings, in the media, etc. What is their purpose? How effective are they with you?
- How could you make your message bolder or add even more impact to what you want to say? Are there others with a similar message to yours? If so, how does this affect your message?
- What will happen when you succeed in getting your message across? What feedback will you need to be sure that you were understood? What will be different for you and around you as a result?

HONE YOUR KEY MESSAGE(S): TAKEAWAY LESSONS

Being able to consider your audience and their needs and being able to focus and remain true to the real intent of your message are critical in effective communication. As you can see from the questions above, this is not about you! It's about your message and what you hope to achieve with it. No matter how difficult or easy the message might be, when you consider your message carefully, you will stand more chance of being understood. I encourage you to practise this exercise often. We all carry messages within us. Learning to say them out loud gives them permission to exist and invites others into our world. It connects us to others. In today's busy world, everyone is short on time and attention. Frequent rehearsals of the Key Message exercise will help you hone your communication skills so that you deliver clear and easily understood messages. Too many people complicate the world and relationships with vagueness, nuances, assumptions and implied statements. The Key Message exercise will help you own your words, connect them with who you really are and help you bridge communication gaps to achieve a high level of success.

34

MINE YOUR PAST SUCCESSFUL STRATEGIES

From the day you were born, you were motivated to thrive – to excel, to be productive and to be the best version of yourself that you can be. In psychological terms, you self-actualize – you perfect and develop; you embark on a journey; you live, experience and continuously try to recreate your life to achieve inner satisfaction.

To achieve anything, you first need to be attracted by it. Something appears along the horizon of your consciousness and your brain responds to it by saying, 'I want that!' or maybe 'I want a version of that!' This might be a certain physical appearance, the sorts of friends you have, the job you hold, the partner you marry, the families you nurture, the success you create, the rewards you collect, awards you earn, and so on.

Think of major achievements as stars you collect over time. The reason for looking at successful goals you chose to pursue is to learn about your own successful strategies for creating positive results which you know already. While the strategy may not be perfect, if you have managed to create success in something, you already have a series of key steps to repeat it or to adopt the strategy for another goal. Conscious knowledge of these strategies will help you to increase your productivity because it will give you effective methods that you can apply to future situations without having to figure out each step from scratch.

The Barrier Gliders exercise is about identifying successful strategies you have used in the past. It will help you uncover what motivates you by examining what has motivated you in the past. As you examine the various barriers you have had to overcome, the exercise should strengthen your resilience in the face of obstacles and help to clarify worthwhile future pursuits.

BARRIER GLIDERS EXERCISE

1. Achievements timeline

Think about your major achievements to date. You may wish to list them in chronological order, mind-map them or draw a trajectory like the one below that makes it easy to capture the time dimension of your key successes (flags).

Notes:

Degree   *1st job*   *Pay rise*   *Promotion*

2. Success strategies

Write down what attracted you to each flag. Note down what you had to do to obtain each flag. List the main points or steps you took for reference.

Notes:

3. **Barrier gliders**
   Think about the obstacles you had to face and overcome;
   how did you manage them? Note down your specific strategies in each case, making sure to capture the details of the
   key steps you took and how you went about each one. How
   long did each take? What has this taught you?

   Notes:

4. **Your motto**
   If there was one sentence to summarize a powerful lesson
   you have learned in terms of achieving what you desire, what
   would it be?

   Notes:

5. **Your future horizon**
   Draw a quick sketch of your timeline going forward. Treat
   this as your best guess for what's to come. What does the
   timeline look like? What sort of goals feature on it? What
   specific successes would you like to see on your horizon?

   Notes:

6. **Future gliders**
   How does your future timeline make you feel? Are you
   excited, scared, surprised? What will it take to make the future
   enjoyable, thrilling and worth every minute? Note down your
   thoughts and ideas for action.

   Notes:

Reflective Questions

- What potential successes, if any, did you pass up in pursuit of yours?
- What helped you and what has hindered you most in your journey?
- Generally speaking, are you getting stronger with time? How can you tell?
- What is the key measure of success in your future timeline?

 MINE YOUR PAST SUCCESSFUL STRATEGIES: TAKEAWAY LESSONS

If you complete this exercise in full, you will no doubt be imbued with admiration for the potential you have to pretty much do anything you set your mind to. You will see that while you might have made mistakes and explored some blind alleys, in the end, when you really wanted something, you eventually got it. Along the way you should have learned loads about what works and what doesn't. Perhaps you notice that some of the strategies you used to succeed, you have repeated in different circumstances. This is natural. They have proven themselves to be effective and, provided they are healthy ways of being in the world with others, keep using them. You might have discovered important trends about the sort of things that attract you, be it people, roles or activities. Maybe it's time you tried something different. In almost all cases when I have done this exercise, people tend to draw a positive trajectory for their future, so if yours is positive, that's great news. This shows you that your brain is naturally optimistic. Deep inside, you know you're capable of many successes. All you have to do is choose to pursue them. Equipped with confidence, skills and clarity about what you want, you are ready to be productive. You are resourceful and capable. And you will succeed!

35

GIVE YOURSELF PERMISSION TO SHINE

The world awaits your purpose being lived and expressed in full. Doing what you were meant to be doing because it's who you are makes productivity easy, helps you experience happiness on a regular basis and helps motivate you and others to further action. Early on in life, many people fall into the trap of fitting into the world, but at some point they begin to notice and feel dissatisfaction if they have made costly compromises. They may become aware of time passing and the cost of not leading a fully satisfying life or not living up to their true potential makes itself felt. While others live their ideas and dreams, they struggle under a cloud of excuses and dreaming of someday. They postpone action and delay making a change to their circumstances. They blame others for their bad luck instead of taking responsibility. Are you one of them? Are you capable of so much more than you're giving at the moment?

Why wait? You too could be shining as brightly as the sun *right now*. True potential is hard to contain. Once you give yourself permission to shine and begin to own your awesome power, you will become unstoppable. Only you can unleash yourself because only you know what you can and want to do. And you need not do it alone. Have faith, others will come to your cause. Your potential has a massive force of passion, drive, energy and pure power. It will naturally attract followers. Are you truly shining right now? This is your chance. You only have this life!

Our minds are wonderfully complex organs. They are not afraid to imagine when given permission and full attention. In fact, they cannot help but imagine. It is only the voice of doubt, the internal critic, which makes people inhibit their own full expression. The Ultimate Unleasher is a leadership development and purpose-finding activity. It is really a permission-giving exercise. You give yourself permission to be the *magnificent person* that you are! People's sense of happiness is directly linked to the degree to which their external, real world matches their internal wish for how things should be. Some people call it a calling; others call it a purpose. Whatever you decide to name it, it is your fountain of ultimate productivity.

ULTIMATE UNLEASHER EXERCISE

1. Think about your entry into this world as a magical moment. Your life is truly your show; your performance. You are a complex, highly gifted individual who is, in fact, immensely powerful.

2. Close your eyes and take yourself to a life you would like to live today if you were truly playing full out and felt uninhibited; if you really went for it, whatever that it is for you. It's an amazing world where everything is the way you would wish it to be. It is a perfect fusion of fairness and integrity, and it allows you to walk the earth proud of yourself. You are content and at peace. You exude satisfaction and you are an inspiration to those around you. You are generous and kind. Those that know you are delighted to be your friends and wish to emulate you. Others have heard of you and wish they too could know you.

3. Get in touch with your own magnificence – your inner being and potential change maker. Feel the power you hold spread through you into your household, your place of work, your community. Let it spill out into the world. You might have experienced surges of it or glimpses, either now or in the past. If so, you know what I'm talking about. If not, look at your best moments in life and start there.

 Reflective Questions

- What do you look like unleashed? What will you see/ experience when you truly unleash yourself?
- What are you able to do/want to do when you're in that state?
- What, if anything, would keep you from it?
- What do you need to support you to be at your best? Who will you enlist in your cause, and how, to help you unleash yourself or stay in your best zone?

GIVE YOURSELF PERMISSION TO SHINE: TAKEAWAY LESSONS

The Ultimate Unleasher illustrates two fundamental lessons about your potential and productivity. First, you have come equipped with an inner calling, a vision of your possibility and greatness that you can tap into for inspiration, learning and guidance, either on your own or with the help of a development professional, mentor or good friend. What you have probably captured represents one vision of your desires and goals and, whether you know it or not, you are already working towards it. All we can do is help accelerate this process or help you to make a larger difference.

If you jotted down your ideas or vision, you will notice that what you unleashed is underpinned by your values, beliefs and deep yearnings. By giving yourself permission to imagine it, you have accessed and distilled a piece of your innermost self and you have brought it out into something concrete and specific. It is a starting point, but not a complete picture. It's a clue. It might be foggy or incomplete. It may require incubation. That is often the case, in fact. With time, however, it will get clearer and crisper. This is where working with a coach can be hugely helpful.

Hopefully you also noticed that only you can take action and make the vision a reality. It is up to you. You can wait or you can start today. Remember, people work best in bursts of activity punctuated by lags of recovery, reflection, assessment and learning. Many steps people choose to take towards realizing their visions will be short, energetic, purposeful actions that create results, build momentum and inner confidence. They create small changes that, over time, amount to significant shifts.

So work with what you know and stay curious. Allow yourself to unleash in the world. By doing so, you will inspire others to unleash too. You will develop great satisfaction and inner peace. You will be highly productive on a daily basis. The world is waiting and you're waiting too. Free yourself and unleash!

36

FIND THE TRIBE THAT WILL HELP YOU SOAR

One of the basic needs of humans is to be loved and accepted, to be part of a group and to belong. A tribe is a network of people who share common interests and values. Productive people all have their tribes – people who inspire them, people they connect with, learn from and trust. People in your tribe will appreciate you, support you and generally want you to succeed. They will help you get through difficulties and offer you motivation at crucial times. These are people you enjoy and have fun with and who speak your language, share your aspirations or who make perfect soaring mates. Your tribe makes you feel good about who you are, encourages your talents and helps validate you. Having a tribe helps you to be productive faster and on a greater scale. They really are the people you can't afford to be without.

You might have already found members of your tribe, or maybe you are still searching. Your tribe might include your clients, friends, family members and people who share your interests or passions. Today's interconnected world allows us to connect with people across countries and cultures. Rest assured, your tribe is out there. Depending on your role and aspirations, your tribe might be small, medium-sized or very large. If you're a team leader it might be your whole team. If you're a CEO, perhaps it's all your employees. If you're a business owner, maybe it's every existing and potential client. People in your tribe allow you to be at your most productive. They give you ideas, share insights and collaborate with you. You co-create together. Therefore, the time you spend together is rewarding and highly worthwhile. It helps you achieve more than you could ever achieve alone. The energy you invest in your tribe is worth it.

The Tribe Nourishment exercise is designed to help you systematically identify characteristics of your tribe so that you can grow your support base and thrive. It will also help you identify clues about where and how to identify people you want to connect with. Time is precious. Be aware of people that drain your energy and time. Spend it with those that help you soar.

TRIBE NOURISHMENT EXERCISE

1. Think about people in your life right now who you really connect with. People whose company you seek to recharge and nourish your dreams, ideas and goals. People who help you get things done, raise your standards, reassure you, challenge and believe in you. People who set you on fire with enthusiasm, possibility, drive and really help you to be your most productive.

2. Sketch a diagram of your tribe to help you visualize what you have already or how you might strengthen it.

Notes:

3. For each person in your tribe, note down the key role or roles this person or people play. So, for example, your motivated employees/successful clients might give you confidence that you're doing things right. Others might be great companions, champions, energizers or thinking partners. One way or another, each of these people helps you succeed. You may wish to group some people for convenience.

Notes:

4. Note down the common characteristics that connect you with your tribe. Is it a similar purpose, approach, way of being, interest or values? What other characteristics would you like

your tribe to have that reflect what you value and aspire towards? Note what's missing, if anything, so you can focus on finding a way to add it. Is there another tribe that offers it?

Notes:

5. What is the nature of the nourishment that your tribe gives you? Are there other sources of it? If so, are you making the most of them? What do you offer your tribe that attracts them? What more could you offer that would benefit everyone?

Notes:

6. How did you meet the people you consider part of your tribe now? What strategies proved most effective? How can you use the same strategy to meet other like-minded people that will nourish you?

Notes:

7. Look at the people you drew or listed in this exercise. Are there specific individuals to whom you owe special gratitude? If so, make a point of telling them.

Reflective Questions

- How does your tribe affect your aspirations and goals? Are the existing connections likely to last or is the tribe transient?
- How do you communicate with your tribe? Do they know what's important to you, what you need and what you can offer? If not, how could you ensure this is the case?
- What activities or events might you consider organizing or taking part in to maintain and strengthen your tribe? This could be to strengthen existing bonds, expertise, collaboration, etc.

 ## FIND THE TRIBE THAT WILL HELP YOU SOAR: TAKEAWAY LESSONS

Your tribe is key to your success. These people are your anchors and your wings. Make sure you make time for them. Share your passion and generosity with them. Be kind to them. They are your allies and fellow travel companions. I hope that doing this exercise has helped you understand the many ways your tribe helps you succeed and what else you might need to nourish and sustain you going forward. Always look for people that help you grow, raise your standards, challenge and inspire you and who are there to help when needed. Be the same to them. Help them achieve their goals. Motivate them. Celebrate your mutual successes together and share learning about your setbacks. Thank and acknowledge the massive impact these people have on your life and you on theirs. Enthusiasm, productivity and success are contagious. Be the spark!

WHAT DOES TRUE PRODUCTIVITY FEEL LIKE?

Have you ever experienced a moment when you were totally in the zone? A time when you felt in control, had a sense of inner delight and satisfaction, where the results you achieved were in line with your aspirations and you seemed to have a sense of inner peace and contentment as well as a feeling that, at that moment, you were a magnificent human being. All of your energy, purpose and motivation aligned and you were able to give something or someone all you had. You did your work efficiently and somehow, perhaps in spite of the levels of work involved, you didn't mind your work. It energized you and gave you a sense of freedom: a sense of immense possibility. In that moment you were what many people in my world of coaching and leadership development call 'on purpose'. Unlike the word 'purpose', which means a final goal or objective to be achieved, 'on purpose' refers to a continuous process of being just where you need to be, doing what you need to be doing, achieving what you want and need to achieve and living the life you're meant to be living. When this occurs, we can enjoy the present moment and take greater advantage of the opportunities and possibilities that the world gives us to enjoy life with ease and happiness. Almost everyone I have ever met has had such moments. Some have them often. They have learned or figured out how to do that. It is but a skill that you can and should develop to be in control of your own destiny.

UNLEASHING YOURSELF BY DESIGN INSTEAD OF BY ACCIDENT REQUIRES A GREAT DEAL OF SELF-KNOWLEDGE, HONESTY AND CRITICAL THINKING SKILLS

Every person makes a number of fresh starts in life and work. Perhaps things don't work out, or aspirations become greater. However you are guided in life, if your actions fail to be informed by self-knowledge, you may simply end up with another false start. This is not necessarily bad. All results give you feedback and help you to learn – from the job you might have failed to get or the relationship that may not have worked out, to all the successes you have had in the past.

The knowledge you acquire through these experiences happens to come rather passively – we tend not to set out to discover it on purpose. Developing greater awareness and insight into your potential and beginning to think critically about your actions speeds up productivity and releases the tension of chasing goal after goal. This is why coaches, therapists and wise mentors and friends all have their role in our lives. It is through both self-reflection and dialogue that we discover purpose and happiness.

Knowing what you want to create and owning your actions is important because it allows you to focus attention and energy in a specific area that will connect with the rational and emotional parts of you. The mind is good at following the heart's plan. When the rational (mind), the emotional (heart) and the visceral (gut) energies align and unite in you, your power and productivity is transformed into a life force. You take purposeful action, you can think clearly and you create fantastic results. Your mind becomes focused like a missile. You can tap into your total resourcefulness of ideas, inspiration, passion and knowledge and you go about obtaining what's missing, whether this is additional skills or resources from people that can help you. Others support you, as they can't resist the clarity of your vision, your commitment and your passion for creating what you believe in. As they witness your happiness and excitement and begin to see your positive intentions, you ignite the sense of possibility in them. You unleash and you lead!

UNLEASHING YOURSELF IS KEY TO PRODUCTIVITY AND YOU CAN DO IT!

The people around us that seem happy and content and who appear to be getting things done and yet still have time to enjoy life, are simply clearer about what they want and are not afraid to commit to it in full. Things do not happen to them by accident. Productive people take purposeful action or work on conditions that will allow action to be taken. They are not afraid to ask. They question. They take an active role in the creation of results. Productive organizations are the same. When all employees understand the business, know and are allowed to communicate ideas and take action, they feel engaged and produce better results.

Almost anything can be done in today's world. We are surrounded by technology to connect us with the whole world and put top talent and experts at arm's reach. All we have to do is be clear about what we want to achieve or to join and actively support someone else's vision when it is a good one. Experiencing happiness means we are left able to add to the happiness of the world around us at a time when this is most needed. What we want is lots and lots of truly productive people: people who are authentic and ready to live their lives to their full potential; people who respect their own needs and those of others; proactive workers; citizens; community members; friends and partners.

FINAL NOTE

A friend of mine once said to me, 'it is time you unleashed yourself on this world' and I wondered what that would be like and what exactly I would be unleashing. I realized I was not alone in that quest, though our conversations had begun a journey of self-discovery and learning that has helped me and those I work with grow. Lots of people choose or settle into being less than their full potential. They pile on lots of activities to be busy. Many claim they can't help it. That they wish things were different, though they often hope they don't really need to change. Some are ready to shift but not sure how, while a few become aware of what they really want yet are filled with doubt as to whether they can bring it about. Almost every person I work with wants to be happier, whatever that term means to him or her. In my experience, I have come to believe that one definition of happiness is holistic productivity satisfied.

As a person, I have a funny sense of impatience. Both of my grandparents died in their fifties, so I often feel that I am working against the clock of life as we know it, though I expect and take action to help me live to a very old age and be healthy. The awareness that as people – individually and collectively – we stand to make a big difference in this world and that we create our own destiny has come to me through life experiences, relationships, learning, reflection and working with myself and others. As a trained neuroscientist, coach and educator, I have the pleasure of working with incredible people in order to help them realize their ambitions.

Feeling alive, passionate, making things happen and helping people around me create lives that are more balanced and fulfilling has become my purpose. I can never get enough of the feeling of enchantment as I speak with another person and see within them so much potential. People and organizations inspire me. The quest to help others unleash their talents and create great places in which to work has led me to study and work with people to help find and bring that potential into its full existence, not someday but now. To unleash it and let it play.

I hope that as you work through the various exercises, you will be inspired to aim for the things you desire most and that you return to the relevant exercises when you need them and learn continuously. I invite you to share this material and your learning with others. The world can't wait for all the wonderful things each of us has the capacity to create. We are living in a period of unprecedented change, with so much potential for creating a better, fairer and more inclusive world. Having more people living more productive lives will be enjoyable and beneficial to us all.

I look forward to hearing about your progress.

With warmest wishes
Magdalena

FURTHER READING

While I hope that working with my book will get you to take action, people often query me for book recommendations. Below is a short list of books I would whole-heartedly recommend to readers of *Get Productive!* They have influenced my own thinking, productivity and how I show up and I regularly give them to others as presents.

Sumo – Paul McGee
Time Power – Brian Tracey
The 7 Habits of Highly Effective People – Stephen Covey
The Artist's Way – Julia Cameron
Taming Your Gremlin – Rick Carson
28 Days to Discover the Real You – Dennise Linn
Super Coach – Michael Neill
Synchronicity: The Inner Path of Leadership – Joseph Jaworsky
Leadership and Self-deception – Arbinger Institute
Leadership from the Inside Out – Kevin Cashman
The Four Elements – Michael Ruiz
The Strength Finder – Tom Rath
Never Hit a Jellyfish with a Spade – Guy Browning
Oh, the Places You Will Go – Dr Seuss

THANKS

I strongly believe that people come into our lives for a reason. So before mentioning any names, which would be a book in itself, I would like to express my thanks to all those who have shown up in my life up to this moment. I thank you, celebrate you and wish you well in your life's journeys.

There are however a number of individuals in my recent past that have truly contributed, shaped, changed and generally improved my life for the better and I would like to give them space here as through their way of being they have helped me show up better!

On the work front I would like to thank my current Deputy Rector Prof. Stephen Richardson for his support and for believing in my ideas for what we can create at Imperial along with Kim Everitt, Deputy HR Director. A big thank you to everyone in my Learning and Development team: Sarah Couter, Steve Rathborn, Judy Barnett, Jean-David Rouah, Fiona Richmond, Lindsay Comalie, Tammy Wong, Eric Miranda, Rosie Heart and Martyn Casey. You are a great bunch of people to work with: professional, inspiring and human. Thank you to many other individuals at Imperial for your energy and support. You are my daily enhancers.

With regards to this book, I would like to thank the following people: Alison Hodge a great friend and mentor who helped me to develop some patience for the creative process of not rushing things and Rita McGee for being a friend and mentor who has been there for me at critical turning points. I'd like to thank Rona Steinberg and

Holly Crane, who are both excellent coaches and friends, for their support, kind hearts and unconditional love, and my coach Suzy Grieves for her positive energy and big-leaping philosophy. Writing a first book is daunting and I would like to say thanks to a few critical friends and professional colleagues whose opinion I trusted and valued and who read the material from this book at the very start, gave useful feedback and encouragement that helped me to keep going: Gabriela Albescu, Steven D'Souza, Sarah Couter, Jon Tucker, Tracey Ward, Anna Korre and Bachir Taouti. Thank you guys!

I would like to thank Guido and Ulrike Fuchs for their help with putting me in touch with the Wiley business books team. Big thanks to Iain Campbell for believing in the idea for this book from the start, to Jonathan Shipley my editor for working with me to create this product and to Jenny Ng for her excellent assistance on text and images as well as everyone within the Wiley Capstone team.

Thank you to all my coaching clients and workshop attendees. You have given me lots of ideas and inspiration over the years and I feel privileged to have met you and worked with you. Thank you to all my dear friends. You are my adopted family. Thank you to Stefan Maier for the gift of true friendship and love. Finally a large thanks to two people who have given me magic sparkle, writing feathers, critical thinking hats and generally never fail to inspire me with their generosity, support, love and kindness: Tracey Ward and Jill Hough. You are angels in disguise.

Thank you to those not mentioned explicitly here. You live in my heart.

Finally thank you to my reader, for picking this book and for allowing me to touch your life in some way at a distance. Any benefits you will gain from what I have to share will give me great joy and makes projects like this book worth it!

ABOUT THE AUTHOR

Magdalena Bak-Maier was born in Poland and moved to the USA as a child. She grew up in New York as an inquisitive, hardworking immigrant kid fascinated by the people she met in the Big Apple. She obtained a BSc in Neuroscience from New York University followed by a PhD from Caltech in Developmental Neurobiology. Following a successful career in research, deciphering the mechanisms that help wire brains in early development, Magdalena decided to combine logic with emotion and her passion for developing people. She made a move to Organizational Development developing academic leaders and staff at Bristol University.

In 2007 she embarked on professionalizing her coaching skills as a Master Coach. She realized that she was capable of unlocking potential talent for leadership and top-level performance within the context of different organizational cultures by merging what she knew about how brains work and coaching theory. She became certified in Myers Briggs Type Indicator (MBTI) and achieved full accreditation as a Neuro Linguistic Programming (NLP) Practitioner. She then studied with the Coach Training Institute (CTI) and Arbinger Institute and is a full member of the Association for Coaching. She continues to regularly deepen her facilitation, mediation and coaching practice through reading, reflection, journaling, supervision, discussion and teaching and she is an active contributor to the Imperial Coaching Academy.

Today, Magdalena works with highly intelligent and creative professionals including renowned scientists, artists and global social entrepreneurs within top-tier organizations. She merges logic with emotion to inspire, lead and facilitate personal and organizational change. Magdalena's highly effective productivity training has been sought to develop staff within Imperial College London and the Imperial Business School, KLM/AirFrance, Ashoka (a non-profit organization supporting the field of social entrepreneurship), the London School of Economics and Royal College of Music.

Magdalena has worked with notable people on developing inspiring pitches and talks (G8 summit, World Economic Forum e.t.c.), bringing leadership visions to life and collaborative idea generation events that bring together people from different disciplines to solve Grand Challenges. She is a creator and leader of numerous group workshops and personal development journeys that touch the soul. She helps to bring out people's true calling and to build their confidence and momentum so that they can undertake the challenge of showing up authentically and making things happen. For the past four years, she has focused much of her attention on developing leadership capability and unleashing talent at Imperial College London as well as developing further coaching mastery by working as a personal coach to a diverse set of leaders, professionals and change makers. She has an ongoing interest in how people learn and mine the power of their own minds, as well as social entrepreneurship. Magdalena is a Fellow of the RSA and lives in London.

You can find out more about Magdalena's work and life at www.maketimecount.com